Piotr Socha * Monika Utnik-Strugała

The Book of Dirt

A smelly history of human hygiene

T&H

Contents

I'd like to dedicate this book to everyone who built, designed and engineered the water and sewer networks. Their work makes our lives so much easier and more pleasant, even though we often don't notice it. I can easily imagine a world without generals or famous leaders, or soldiers carrying guns. I find it much harder to imagine living without properly working toilets, sewers or running water. While a world without war would undoubtedly be a better one, a world without these comforts, which we so often take for granted, would definitely be a worse place to live in.

– Piotr Socha

For billions of people on earth, washing our hands, brushing our teeth, taking a shower or a bath, using deodorant and going to the toilet are such common events that we hardly think about them. But this wasn't always the case. Nor is it true all over the world.

For instance, the ancient Greeks and Romans loved to spend time in public bath houses. However, when the plague reached Europe in the 14th century, some Christian people started to believe that washing was bad for the body – and that idea stuck around for hundreds of years. In the meantime, medieval Muslim people happily visited public bath houses and many Japanese people were shocked by the dirtiness of the Portuguese traders who reached their islands in the 16th century.

In the 19th century, the scientist Louis Pasteur proved that dirt is full of dangerous bacteria. People then started to realize that clean water doesn't cause diseases – in fact, it can help to fight against them. But change happened slowly. In 1882, when the study of hygiene was first taught in French schools, the only piece of advice was to wash the parts of your body that people can see – your face and hands.

However, as the medieval philosopher Bernard of Clairvaux once wrote, 'when everyone stinks, no one smells.' In most cases, our approach to hygiene depends on the culture we live in. For example, for a 17th-century French gentleman of the upper classes, being clean meant changing his shirt, powdering his face and sprinkling on some perfume – but washing was not thought necessary.

Much more recently, when the COVID-19 pandemic happened, we were all told how to wash our hands properly, and hand sanitizer and toilet paper vanished from shop shelves. It became clear that dirt is not just an interesting subject, it's also an extremely important one.

When everyone stinks, no one smells.

St Bernard
(11th–12th centuries)

A clean body and clothes hide an unclean soul.

St Paula of Rome
(4th–5th centuries)

He that is washed in Christ does not need to wash again.

St Jerome
(4th–5th centuries)

Wash your hands often, your feet rarely and your head never.

English proverb
(17th century)

No hairs sprouting from your nose. Don't let your breath turn sour. And don't smell like a shepherd or his flock.

Ovid, Roman poet
(1st century)

There's character in soap and water.

The sick may take baths whenever advised, but the healthy, and especially the young, should be given permission less readily.

What's the cleanest leaf in the forest?

Holly – because nobody dares wipe their bum on it!

A medieval joke

St Benedict of Nursia
(5th–6th centuries)

Slogan of the American Cleanliness Institute (1920s)

Wash before bed, you'll soon be dead!

I wash once a month whether I need it or not.

What can I say of those whose robes smell good, whose shirt sleeves are so white they could wipe their face and hands on them, who eat fragrant herbs to freshen their breath, yet their clothes are made of the blood and sweat of the poor?

A truly virtuous woman has no wish to spoil her natural beauty.

Queen Elizabeth I of England (16th–17th centuries)

Maciej of Książa, preacher (15th century)

A bath should be taken every spring, at the time of the yearly bloodletting.

To treat a case of infected teeth, take some hemp seed, cook it in a new pot until it starts to peel, then add nine hot stones. Lean over the steam and the bugs will fall out.

Thomas Turner, English shopkeeper (17th century)

St Jerome (4th–5th centuries)

How dirty your hands are, my lady!

What would you say if you saw my feet?

Dirt is a second skin.

Mary Wortley Montagu, British aristocrat (17th–18th centuries)

Szymon of Łowicz (16th century)

Bathing, except for vital medical reasons, is not only unnecessary, but very harmful to men.

Theophraste Renaudot, French doctor (1655)

I take after my father, I smell of armpits.

Louis XIII, King of France (17th century)

It's much better to watch a patient, damp with sweat, dry out in the warmth of his bed, and better for the patient himself to bear the smell of sweat for a few days, than to change his bedsheets and in so doing bring about his death.

Isbrand van Diemerbroeck, Dutch doctor (17th century)

No one in my family ever took a bath!

Countess de Pange, French aristocrat (19th century)

Water takes it out of you.

Today I took a shower: it is quite a good rehearsal for purgatory. You stand naked in a small underground place, and there is a hose of hot water, which a woman points wherever you choose. This state, in which you have scarcely a fig leaf to cover you, is very humiliating.

Clean underwear in abundance is worth more than all the baths in the world.

Charles Perrault, French fairytale writer (16th–17th centuries)

Wash too much and you'll wash yourself away.

The Marquise de Sevigne, French aristocrat (1676)

Bathrooms are only for servants.

Lady Mariabella Fry (early 20th century)

When the people become friends of cleanliness, they will also soon become the friends of order and discipline.

Never allow yourself more than one bath a month. The taste for sitting down in a bathtub encourages a certain laziness and softness that ill suits a woman.

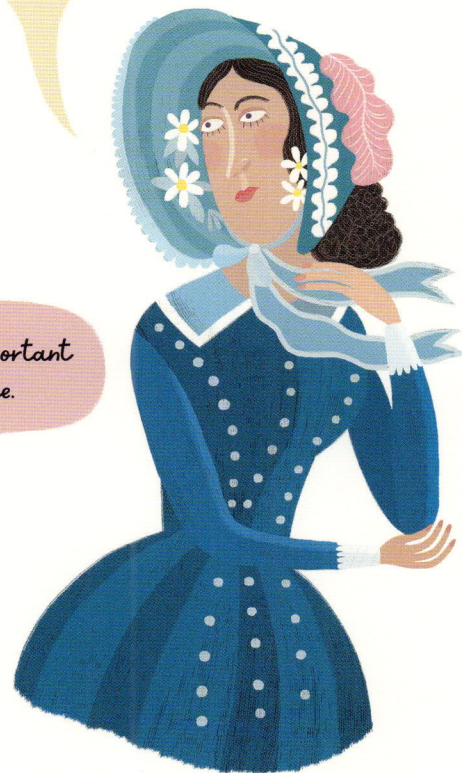

French Council for Health (1840)

A weekly bath for every German!

Oskar Lassar, German doctor (mid-19th century)

Sanitation is more important than independence.

Mahatma Gandhi, Indian activist (1925)

Countess Drohojowska, Polish aristocrat (19th century)

Cleanliness is next to godliness.

Charles Wesley, English theologian (18th century)

A woman's arm! Poets have sung of its grace; artists have painted its beauty. It should be the daintiest, sweetest thing in the world. And yet, unfortunately, it isn't, always.

Streptocock-Gee to Banbury-T, to see a fine bathroom and W.C.

Aldous Huxley, 'Brave New World' (1932)

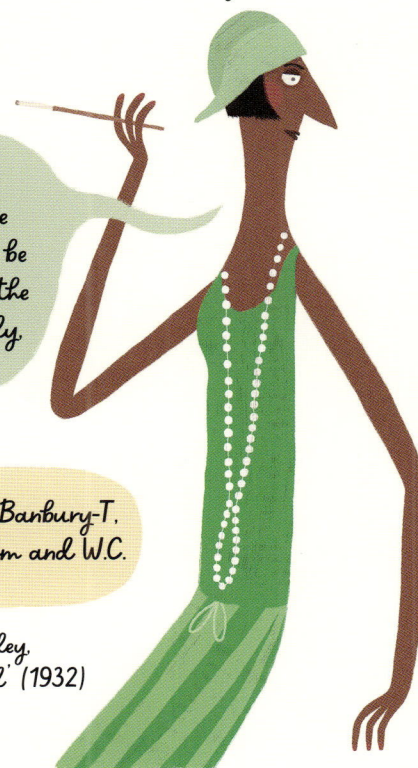

Advert for Odorono deodorant (1919)

Dirty words?

It's easy to tell how important dirt and cleanliness are from all the phrases and expressions they appear in. If we want to offend someone, we might call them 'dirtbag', 'slobby' or 'snot-nosed'. If we want to speak negatively about something, we can call it 'filthy', 'crappy' or 'rubbish'. We might also say that something stinks (if it seems suspicious), someone needs to clean up their act (they have to behave better), their hands are dirty (if they've done something dishonest) or they're doing someone's else dirty work (if they do dishonest things for somebody else). Some of these expressions have interesting stories behind them. Here are just a few.

Money doesn't stink – this proverb means that money is always welcome, regardless of where it comes from.

The saying goes back to the Roman emperor Vespasian. The story goes that, in order to make more money for the Roman state, Vespasian decided to introduce a tax on urine. This seems like a strange thing to do, but pee was used by leather-makers to tan animal hides, so it was quite valuable. When his son Titus protested, Vespasian waved a coin under his nose and asked him if he was offended by the smell. Titus said no. The emperor replied that the coin came

from the urine tax, and added: *Pecunia non olet* – Latin for 'money doesn't stink'.

To wash one's hands of something – to refuse to get involved with something or to claim no responsibility for it.

This expression comes from the Gospel of St Matthew in the Bible. The Roman governor Pontius Pilate was made to put Jesus on trial but did not believe he was guilty. Seeing that the leaders of the Jewish temple wanted to punish Jesus, Pilate sentenced Jesus to death. However, he wanted to distance himself from the decision because he didn't want to take responsibility for killing

an innocent man. Following an ancient Jewish custom, he washed his hands in a bowl of water, which was meant to cleanse him symbolically. 'I am innocent of the blood of this just person,' he said.

Today, when we say that someone is washing their hands of something, we mean that we think they're avoiding responsibility for it.

Money-laundering – to launder money is to take money gained from illegal activities, such as smuggling or selling drugs, and swap it with legal money.

We probably owe this saying to the gangster Al Capone. In the 1920s, he was the

leader of Chicago's Mafia, a criminal organization that made and sold alcohol, even though it was banned in the USA at the time. At the same time as running their criminal operations, the Mafia also owned legal businesses, such as laundries. They added the profits from the sale of alcohol to their honest income in order to hide where it came from.

Soap opera – a dramatic story told in a series of episodes, usually on TV, but originally on the radio.

This expression comes from America in the 1930s, when the first radio dramas were broadcast. They were given the ironic name 'operas' because they were the opposite of sophisticated musical operas. The term 'soap' came from the fact that these shows were often sponsored by soap companies, who wanted to encourage the many women who listened to the dramas to buy their products to clean their homes.

Don't wash your dirty linen in public – you shouldn't talk openly about family matters or private subjects, especially if they're embarrassing or awkward. The ancient Romans had a similar expression, 'it's an ill bird that fouls its own nest',

carelessly that you lose something good at the same time.

It seems that this phrase first came into use in German, and then was borrowed by English. It's a striking way to make someone focus on what's really important.

To get the wrong end of the stick – to misunderstand something.

One possible explanation for this expression is that it comes from Roman times, when people would wipe their bottoms using a sponge on a stick called a *xylospongium* (see p. 141). These sticks were shared by everyone at the public toilets. It certainly wouldn't have been very nice to pick one up from the wrong end!

To spend a penny – to pee.

Because going to the toilet is often considered a little bit embarrassing, not everyone likes to talk about it openly. Instead, they often use phrases like this one to avoid mentioning the topic. It comes from the times when it cost one penny to use a public toilet.

Throw enough dirt and some will stick – if someone becomes the subject of enough lies or gossip, people will start to believe it, even it's not really true.

Scandalous stories and secrets are often referred to as 'dirt' in English, appearing in phrases like 'dishing the dirt' (spreading gossip) or 'digging up dirt' (finding out someone's secrets to make them look bad).

meaning that you shouldn't gossip about your own family or background.

What does doing laundry have to do with talking in public? It probably comes from the times when people would wash clothes outside, in streams and rivers. It was the perfect occasion to meet your neighbours and have a bit of a gossip.

To come up smelling of roses – to come out of a difficult situation looking better than might be expected.

This modern phrase may be a short version of a longer, older saying – 'to fall in dirt and come up smelling of roses'!

Don't throw the baby out with the bathwater – don't make the mistake of getting rid of something bad so quickly or

Looking good in ancient Egypt

Keeping clean was incredibly important in ancient Egypt. Not only did the ancient Egyptians think that good hygiene was a way to stay healthy but they believed people needed to stay clean in the afterlife as well. This is why archaeologists have found beauty products and toiletries buried inside the pyramids.

The Egyptians would sometimes wash several times a day. Staying clean was especially important for priests, but every house had a basin and jug for water and a bowl for washing feet. The wealthiest people also had separate bathrooms, where they washed in tubs or shallow pools, and their servants would shower them with water brought straight from the Nile. Poorer people could bathe in the river, but they had to watch out for crocodiles!

Every day on waking, Egyptians washed their entire body. They cleaned their hands, face and feet before every meal, after eating, on returning home and before going to bed. After bathing, they applied a cream to their skin, which kept it protected from the sun and also helped to keep insects away.

They also cleaned their teeth every morning with toothpaste and a brush. Yes, the ancient Egyptians had toothbrushes! According to one recipe that has been discovered, early Egyptian toothpaste was made of mint, salt, pepper and ground dried flowers, which turned into a paste when it mixed with the spit inside your mouth. The first Egyptian toothbrush was just a twig with frayed ends, but later they began to use real brushes made from thin strips of papyrus.

To make it easier to stay clean, the Egyptians removed their body hair (see p. 67). They also took care of their nails, which they filed and cut with special scissors.

As well as keeping clean, the people of the Nile wanted to smell nice. Egyptian perfumes often came in the form of creams. These were made from a mixture of animal fat, tree sap, cinnamon, cardamom, flowers and herbs. They also used a deodorant made from a paste that included ground-up nuts, tree bark, ostrich eggs and tortoise shells, which they spread on their bodies to soak up sweat. The Egyptians worried about bad breath too – they sucked sweets made from resins, cinnamon and honey to make sure they smelled fresh.

And the ancient Egyptians didn't stop there. Did you know that ancient Egyptian women invented the first tampons? They were made from softened, rolled-up pieces of papyrus.

Soap and skincare

Soap, shampoo, face cream, make-up – these everyday inventions have long and colourful histories.

In Mesopotamia, people probably washed with a pulp made of tallow and ash. The ancient Egyptians (see p. 19) used blends of animal and plant fats to clean themselves. The Greeks and Romans (see p. 31) used a mixture of olive oil, dust and sand – they spread it over themselves and then used a blunt metal blade called a strigil to scrape everything off, dirt included.

Bars of soap were apparently invented by the Phoenicians – these were made of goat fat and lye from wood ash. In the Arab world (see p. 43), soap was made from olive oil. In Europe, early soap-makers set up business in Spain, Italy and France. The most highly valued was soap produced in the Castile region of Spain. But this soap was very expensive and a long time passed before it was widely used.

In ancient Egypt, everyone wore make-up – men and women, children and adults, the rich and the poor. It wasn't just a form of decoration, it was thought to have magical powers of protection.

The most common kind of Egyptian make-up was thick dark eyeliner. This was thought to protect the person wearing it, and symbolized the eye of the goddess Hathor or the gods Ra or Horus. The lines were drawn using kohl, which is still used

in some places in the world today. It is a mixture of antimony (a silvery metal), lead, copper oxide, burnt almonds, ash, ochre (a reddish clay), malachite (a green mineral) and chrysocolla (a turquoise mineral). The powdered ingredients were mixed with fat on a special palette before being applied. The Egyptians also used face powder and stained their lips red and their cheeks pink using a lipstick made of ochre, fat and resin.

They also took great care of their skin. They made creams and lotions out of wax, honey and milk, as well as mineral oils and plant and animal fats – including hippopotamus fat. Lots of their ingredients, such as honey, milk, castor oil or marigold flowers, are still found in cosmetics today.

It is believed that the Egyptian queen Cleopatra took regular baths in donkey's milk. To prepare one bath for her, her servants had to milk seven hundred donkeys. The Roman doctor Galen also says that she invented a treatment to prevent hair loss for her lover, the Roman emperor Julius Caesar.

Its ingredients included roasted mice and horses' teeth as well as bear fat and the bone marrow from deer.

The women of ancient Greece and Rome were fond of beauty products too. They wore kohl, blusher and eyeshadow. They made blusher from lichens, ochre or plant roots and they created creams with unusual ingredients such as sheep fat, powdered deer antlers and lizard poo. They also made face masks using birds' nests and made their skin pale with toxic white lead (see p. 93).

Although some of the recipes for ancient make-up may seem rather odd to us, it's worth remembering that some modern beauty products contain ingredients that sound as if they'd be more at home in a witch's cauldron than a beauty salon. These include fish scales, oil from turtle eggs, snake venom and snail slime!

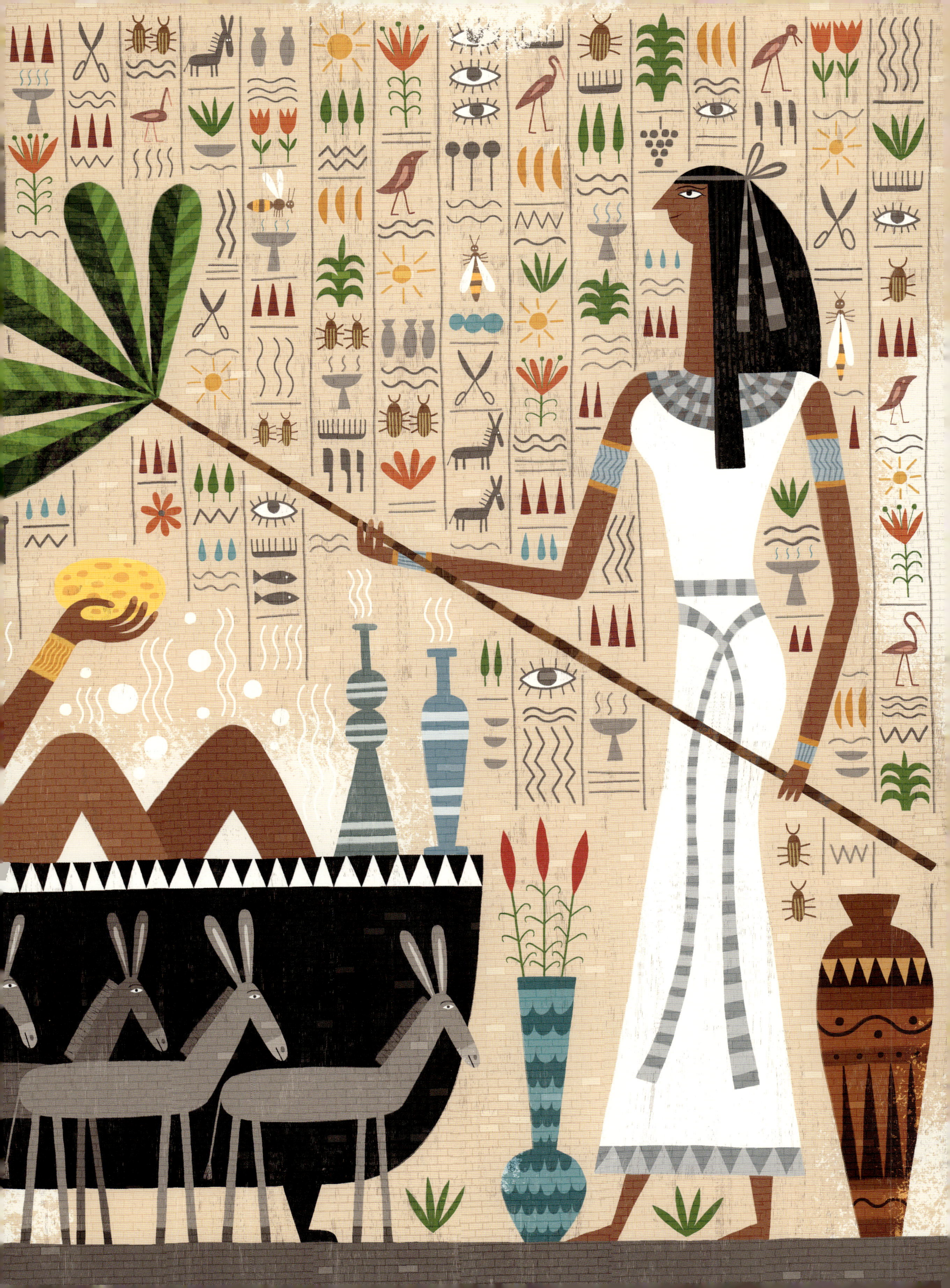

Where do you bathe, Marcus?

For the ancient Romans, bathing was a social activity. They spent a lot of their free time at public bath houses. Even though the wealthiest families had private bathrooms at home, they often preferred to wash in town, with everyone else.

Not far from Termini train station in Rome is the Basilica of St Mary of the Angels and of the Martyrs, designed by Michelangelo. It's a huge building, which makes anyone entering feel as tiny as an ant. The church was constructed just over four hundred years ago, but its vaults and front are over 1,700 years old. Michelangelo built the basilica in the ruins of the Baths of Diocletian – an ancient complex of public baths or *thermae*.

When he began work, the baths were in a terrible state and their crumbling walls were overgrown with weeds. Nobody had used them for a long time. Michelangelo, who was fascinated by the beauty of old buildings, decided to preserve as much of

them as possible. Thanks to him, Italians can now pray, marry and have their children baptised in the same space where their ancestors once bathed, exercised and did business deals.

The *thermae* were a bit like a waterpark and spa in one, as well as a place to relax and hold social or business meetings. In the centre were the three bathing rooms: the *tepidarium*, a room with a warm pool, the *caldarium*, where the water in the pool was hot, and the *frigidarium*, where the pool was cold. The floor was warmed from below to make sure each room was the right temperature. That's right, underfloor heating – known as a hypocaust – is an ancient invention! How did it work? The floor was built on posts about 80 centimetres high. A special wood-burning furnace underneath heated the air between the posts.

Everyone could use the Roman public baths: adults and children, free citizens and slaves, men and women. Men usually went in the afternoon and women in the morning. Interestingly, the entry fee for women was sometimes twice as much as for men. But

children could take a dip for free. Soldiers were also allowed free baths.

A visit to the *thermae* usually began with doing exercises. Then you entered the *tepidarium*, to sweat and scrape your skin with a strigil (see p. 23). Next you visited the *caldarium* and finally the *frigidarium*. The last part of a Roman bath was a massage, where olive oil was rubbed into the skin and once again scraped off with the strigil.

Apart from the bathing rooms, bigger Roman baths also had exercise rooms and sports areas. Some had canteens and rooms for playing dice, others even had libraries and lecture halls. It's no wonder that Seneca, the famous philosopher, who lived above a public bathhouse, complained about the constant noise: the splash of water in the pools, the shouts of people watching ball games, the grunts of people exercising, the slapping sound of hands massaging skin, the yelps of people having their armpits waxed (see p. 67), the cries of snack sellers, and plenty of loud conversations and arguments.

The bustling, crowded *thermae* often stayed open until midnight. Rich Romans spent

long hours there, not only bathing and exercising but also doing business, talking politics and debating the future of the country. In ancient Rome, when you met somebody new, it was common to ask 'where do you bathe?', to find out which baths they went to.

In earlier years, when Rome was a republic, the baths were smaller and known as *balneae*. The smallest had just the three bathing rooms. Much grander baths were given the name *thermae*, and were built by the Roman emperors Nero, Trajan, Caracalla and Diocletian. The Baths of Caracalla covered around 12 hectares and could fit six thousand people inside.

The baths built by the emperors were very luxurious. They had marble columns and tiled floors, and were decorated with fountains and statues. A famous statue called *Laocoön and his Sons*, which is now in the Vatican Museum, may have once stood in the Baths of Titus, while the Baths of Caracalla were adorned with the statues of the *Farnese Bull* and *Farnese Hercules*. In addition, the walls and floors were often covered with frescoes and mosaics. Some of these have survived to this day and are a priceless source of information about the daily life of ancient Romans.

Unfortunately, the Roman baths stopped working in the 6th century CE, when the armies of the Goths invaded and destroyed Rome's aqueducts (see p. 40), and very few of them are still standing today. Some of the best-preserved Roman baths are the ones in the city of Bath in England.

Ancient Greece also had public baths, but they were not as fancy as the Roman ones. If you wanted to, you could take a bath (or join a philosophical debate or listen to a lecture) at the gymnasium (see p. 35), which was a sports centre with a field and running track. But the baths in gymnasia were quite small and were only meant for cooling down and washing after training. For the Romans, who built huge bath houses with relatively small exercise areas, physical activity was just a sideshow to the main event of taking a bath.

The watery wonders of Rome

You may be surprised to learn that sewers and waterworks are very old inventions. They existed in ancient Rome, and some of the systems built centuries ago are still working today.

In Rome, not far from the Via Appia, one of the oldest surviving roads of the ancient empire, lies the Aqueduct Park, a huge grassy space filled with stone arches. They may look like the ruined arcades of a huge palace, but they're actually the remains of an ancient water supply system.

Aqueducts (from the Latin *aquae ductus*, 'to lead water') were used to carry water from springs in the mountains and hillsides to fountains, bath houses, public toilets and wealthy homes in Roman towns. The water flowed because the pipes were slightly sloped. To achieve this, they were laid along carefully planned routes. Tunnels were dug through mountains and bridges built over valleys to carry the water. Most waterworks were underground but some parts included huge rows of arches, which could be two or three storeys tall.

The Syrians, Greeks and Phoenicians had built simpler aqueducts before, but it was the Romans who perfected the art. Their waterworks did have one problem, however – the pipes were made of lead, which is very dangerous for humans. Nonetheless, modern experts say that the Romans were harmed much more by the poisonous lead dishes they used for storing and preparing food than by their water pipes.

In the 2nd century CE, Rome was home to around one million people. The city received water from eleven aqueducts, measuring 420 kilometres in total, of which almost 50 kilometres were above ground. Most of the aqueducts were destroyed in the 6th century CE by the Goths, who invaded the Roman empire (see p. 35), but some are still in use today, including the Aqua Marcia and Aqua Virgo. The latter provides water for the famous Trevi fountain, one of Rome's top tourist attractions.

Aqueducts were built wherever the Roman army set foot, in places including France, North Africa and Asia Minor. Some of the arches can still be admired today, including the Pont du Gard near Nîmes in France, and the Aqueduct of Valens in Istanbul, Turkey, which was once part of a network almost 250 kilometres long.

The people of ancient Rome not only had a good water supply, they also had sewage systems. In the Roman Forum, the main city square, close to the ruins of the Basilica Julia, there is a mysterious lead door. When you stand near it, you can hear the sound of rushing water. The door opens onto the main sewer of the ancient capital.

It's called the Cloaca Maxima, which means 'biggest sewer', and it was built in the 7th century BCE. At first it was in the open air, but later, when the stink began to make the Romans' life a misery, it was covered over. It's about 600 metres long, 4 metres high and more than 3 metres wide. A small amount of water still runs through it today, but far less than in the days of the Roman empire.

The Cloaca Maxima did not solve all of Rome's hygiene problems, however, because at night when the public latrines were closed, Romans relieved themselves in chamber pots and poured their contents into the street. But by day, they happily did their business in communal toilets (see p. 110), and then the sewer served its purpose brilliantly. Thanks to this clever sewer system, ancient Rome probably smelled much nicer than European cities in the Middle Ages (see p. 76).

The Romans even had a goddess of sewers, Cloacina. People would pray to her for help when the pipes became blocked, overflowed or even exploded. This sometimes happened because there was no ventilation to release the gases that could build up inside.

Turkish-style baths

After the fall of the Roman Empire, public baths disappeared from European towns. They made a comeback in around the 11th century thanks to the Crusaders. These were Christian knights who set off for Jerusalem on a number of occasions to try to take over the city from Muslim rule. They were called Crusaders because they wore robes with a large cross on them – the word *crucesignatus* means 'marked by the cross'. Although the Crusaders were not able to keep control of Jerusalem after conquering it in the First Crusade, they saw many new things on their journey – including hammams.

In the Islamic world, a hammam is a public steam bath. It usually consists of a changing room, a warm room with hot air, a hot room with humid air, and a cooler resting area. In the warm room, guests get used to the heat and in the next space, they enjoy treatments such as cleansing and massages. The interiors are decorated with colourful mosaics and marble, which heats up quickly and stays hot for a long time. The ceiling of the main room is often a semi-circular dome with lots of small round openings to let in

the daylight. In the middle of the room, there is a large stone platform, sometimes called a belly stone, where guests can lie during their treatments.

Hammams were originally based on Roman baths (see p. 29), but instead of swimming pools, they usually have sinks with taps and running water – the exceptions are baths built close to mineral springs, and Iranian hammams, which had a large, shared heated pool. This was a result of cultural differences – for religious reasons, Muslim people believe that it's better to bathe in running water (see p. 60). Compared to an ancient Roman bath house, it's certainly much more hygienic, too.

Like Roman baths, hammams have always been popular meeting spots. They were used by everyone – rich and poor, old and young, women and men. But men and women were not allowed to bathe together.

Muslim women were particularly fond of hammams. For them, the baths were a bit like a café and a beauty salon in one. Not only did they go there to wash, they could also choose from beauty treatments including hair removal, face masks or creams. Then when they were finished, they could relax and chat over a glass of tea.

To celebrate special occasions, feasts would be held in hammams – sometimes they were very lavish and had live music. Weddings were one such occasion. Nowadays, Muslim brides-to-be often meet their friends at the hammam for a 'bridal bath', which is rather like a hen party.

The Crusaders came across hammams in Turkey, where every town had its own bath house. But the first medieval bath houses built in Europe were much simpler than Turkish ones. They usually had a steam room and another room containing a large round tub of water, large enough to fit six people. In some towns, bath houses were opened in renovated Roman baths, while large open-air swimming pools were built in places close to

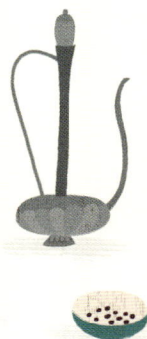

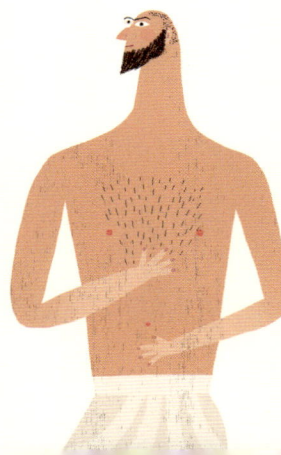

hot springs. Later, European bath houses had special resting areas and private bathrooms. In the late 13th and early 14th centuries, there were around twenty places like this in London and even more in Paris.

Hammams can still be found in Turkey today. You can wash there on your own, take a bath and be washed by someone else, or have a bath and a massage.

When you go to a hammam, you need to take flip-flops and a swimming costume. You can get other items you need for a small fee when you arrive, though Turkish men and women often bring their own equipment with them. You will need a small bucket and a bowl to pour water on yourself, soap, a towel and a special coarse glove. Some people also bring stools and mats to sit on.

In the changing room, you'll be given a large silk or cotton towel (a *peştamal*), usually decorated with a red checked pattern, to wrap around yourself, and clogs if you

didn't bring flip-flops. Then you go into a large room, where the temperature is between 20 and 30°C, and lie down on a bench to warm up your body.

After around twenty minutes, you move to the main room, where it's much hotter and very humid. The Turkish have a saying: *Hamama giren terler*, which means 'if you go to the bath house, you'll get sweaty' – it means that you have to accept the consequences of your actions, rather like the English expression 'if you can't stand the heat, stay out of the kitchen'. Then you lie down on the belly stone and wait until you start to sweat. Next, you rub yourself down with olive soap, rinse off, and scrub off any dry skin with the coarse glove – or in the fancier version, an attendant does it for you.

After the bath is over, you can have a massage, with or without the use of scented oils. Finally, you move to the last room, where you can relax with a cup of very sweet tea.

The smell of saintliness

St Agnes (3rd century) never washed, and St Olympias (4th century) washed only a few times in her life. St Godric (11th–12th centuries) walked from England to Jerusalem without ever washing or changing his clothes. St Francis (12th–13th century) called dirt 'the smelly symbol of holiness', and when he died, his fellow monks said that his spirit visited them and praised their dirty cells. St Hedwig of Silesia (12th–13th century) only cleaned her face with water that other nuns had used to wash their feet, and she dried herself with their dirtiest towels. The Polish writer Jan Długosz wrote that St Kinga (13th century) 'never sought relief in the tub or at the baths, nor did she wash her face with water, except during communion or when in great need'. Why was this?

In the 5th century CE, after the fall of the Roman Empire, a new, thousand-year-long period in European history began. We now call this period the Middle Ages. People stopped worshipping the gods of the ancient world, and social, cultural and political life were dominated by Christianity. Medieval Christian scholars believed that the spiritual world was more important than the physical one. They often saw the physical world as little more than a source of evil.

Humans, they said, are made of an immortal soul that comes from God, and a body, which imprisons the soul and causes it to sin, and which will ultimately be eaten by worms. In that case, why bother taking too

much care of it? They thought it was better to focus on your spiritual needs and devote yourself to prayer.

This is why being spiritually 'clean' was considered more important than being physically clean. Baptism was a symbolic bath for the soul that washed away sin. St Jerome (4th–5th centuries) said that baptism was the only form of washing that people really needed (see p. 64).

Taking a bath was seen not only as unnecessary, but in fact as a source of too much pleasure, probably because it was associated with Roman baths (see p. 29), where people went for fun. Medieval Christians believed the body was the enemy of the soul. Pleasing one was thought to damage the other.

As early as the 2nd century, the author Clement of Alexandria wrote that Christians should not wash for pleasure. In the late 4th century, St Paula of Rome even said that having a clean body was a sign of having an unclean soul. It's no surprise, therefore, that some very strict Christians completely stopped washing or taking care of their bodies completely. This was known as *alousia*, from the Greek for 'being unwashed'. A few went further – not only did they neglect their body, they intentionally made it uncomfortable or even caused it to suffer. Some medieval people wore hair shirts, which were made of scratchy material that was worn over bare skin. And that's only the start of it! St Simeon Stylites (5th century) tied himself up with a rope of thorns, ordered himself to be locked in a barrel and also chained himself to rocks. Eventually, he sat on a small platform on top of a tall pillar of stone and lived there for around forty years. These people who gave up all pleasure and inflicted pain on their bodies were called ascetics.

Of course, not all medieval Christians were ascetics, and the Church didn't encourage people to live in filth. When going to mass, people were meant to wash their hands, feet and face. Before being baptized, they would usually take a bath.

What's more, from around the 11th century onwards, Europe had public bath houses that were very popular (see p. 44). According to some historians, medieval Europeans washed more often than people in the early 20th century.

Even the ascetics themselves didn't think keeping clean was bad, as long as they didn't have to do it themselves. They wanted to imitate Jesus, who washed the feet of his disciples, and they were happy to help others, for instance by nursing and bathing the sick.

Embarrassing bodies

We leave home wearing clothes, we wash naked, we go to the swimming pool in a bathing suit – and it's hard to imagine it any other way! But there are many different ways to dress or undress yourself.

Ancient Greeks not only bathed naked, they also exercised with no clothes on. The name of the place where they trained, the 'gymnasium', comes from the word *gymnos*, which means 'naked'. As for the ancient Romans, they'd never leave home without clothes, but stripped off entirely once they reached the baths (see p. 31).

In medieval Europe, Christians often treated the body with suspicion because it was seen as a source of temptation and sin. It's no wonder people were often embarrassed about their bodies, even when they were alone. It is said that St Olympias always bathed in a shirt to avoid seeing her own body (see p. 49).

Things changed when public bath houses became more popular (see p. 44). In the 15th century in southern Europe, visitors to pools were still quite shy, but in the streets of German towns you could see whole families heading to the baths, half-dressed or even stark naked. At Swiss resorts in Baden, not only did guests wash completely in the nude, there were even little peepholes in the walls between the men's and women's sections so that they could spy on one another.

Another change came in the 17th century. Italian doctors decided to revive the ancient art of balneology, the study of using bathing to treat diseases. Some of the most famous public bath houses – ones that were near mineral springs or hot springs, like in the English city of Bath or the French town of Vichy – were turned into health resorts (see p. 147). Because they were serious centres of medicine, it was no longer appropriate to be naked there.

One English lady who visited the spa at Bath in the late 17th century, described in her diary how women entered the pools wearing stiff linen dresses, while men wore

linen trousers and shirts. Next, everyone took a few dozen steps down into the water, holding onto special rails on the walls. That was as far as they were willing to go.

In the late 17th or early 18th century, it is said that the wife of the English ambassador in Constantinople entered the hammam in Sofia wearing a horse-riding dress. This caused a stir among the Turks bathing there, who were completely naked.

It was not until the 19th century that Europeans began to get more comfortable revealing their bodies when bathing together. This was the time when it became popular for people to spend holidays at the seaside. The long linen dresses and trousers were replaced by swimming costumes. The first swimming costumes for women consisted of a knee-length dress with long sleeves and baggy trousers called bloomers. Men's costumes were a single piece, like a vest and shorts joined together. Over time, these clothes became smaller and smaller and exposed more of the body. Eventually they became the much more skimpy garments we know today.

A clean soul

Many religions pay close attention to hygiene and have detailed rules about what is clean and what is unclean. However, these guidelines aren't always closely connected with actual dirt and the cleansing steps are often symbolic rituals rather than a proper scrub with soap and water. In religious terms, there may be impure foods (like pork in Judaism and Islam), animals (like pigs and dogs in Islam) and activities, and sometimes even groups of people. Washing is often required before prayer, when going to the temple or after committing a sin.

Judaism

In Judaism, impurity is caused by sin, leprosy and coming into contact with corpses but some believe it can also be caused by everyday things like a woman having a period. An unclean person is not allowed to enter the synagogue or touch holy objects. To cleanse themselves, they must bathe in the *mikveh*, a small but deep pool of water, in which they can dip themselves completely. The water must come from a natural source – for instance from a river or stream, or even rainwater – though it can be mixed with tap water. The 'unclean' person must dip under the water three times. This is a purely symbolic act – they have to wash before entering the pool.

Today, *mikvehs* are mostly used by Orthodox Jewish women, who have to cleanse themselves for seven days after their period. Men are not obliged to use the *mikveh*, but some do, for instance before

59

the Sabbath (the day of rest that lasts from Friday evening until Saturday evening) or before holy days, especially Yom Kippur (a day of fasting, penance and reconciliation, which is one of the most important dates in the Jewish calendar). The strictest Jews even cleanse themselves every day, before morning prayers. Using the *mikveh* is also an important step for anyone converting to Judaism and for any devout Jewish woman on the day before her marriage.

Islam

According to the Qur'an, the Muslim holy book, impurity is caused by touching the bottom or private parts. This includes when you're unconscious or asleep, because you don't know what you were doing with your hands. Muslim people make sure that when they wipe themselves or wash their private parts (see p. 145), they only use their left hand. That means they consider it unclean and therefore don't use it for eating food.

In Islam it's also important to be clean before you pray. Muslim people must pray five times each day, but first they perform *wudu* – this means washing your hands, feet and face, dampening your hair and ears, and rinsing your mouth. After sex, childbirth, a period, or converting to Islam, however, you must perform a full-body cleansing called *ghusl*. To perform *ghusl*, you first have to wash your hands three times, then wash your private parts and do *wudu*, then pour water over your head three times, and finally wash the rest of your body, taking care that the water reaches every nook and cranny. When Muslim people die, their bodies are also washed this way. It is also recommended to do *ghusl* before Jumu'ah, the collective prayer that takes place every Friday.

Hinduism

In India, some Hindu people cleanse themselves of sin by bathing in the Ganges, which they believe to be sacred to the goddess Ganga. The entire length of the Ganges is holy, but some parts are more popular than others. One of the most popular places of pilgrimage is the city of Varanasi. It has many large stone steps called ghats, which lead straight into the water, and these are where devotees come to bathe. Every day, around 60,000 people bathe here. Every twelve years, a holy festival called Kumbh

Mela takes place in Allahabad, with pilgrims coming to bathe in the water together. It is the biggest religious festival in the world – 100 million people attended the celebrations in 2013.

Devotees believe that if they die in Varanasi, and their body is cremated and their ashes cast into the Ganges, they will be freed from the cycle of reincarnation – this means that they won't be born again in another body. The bodies of the dead are cremated on a ghat, not far from where the ritual baths take place. The river is also used by poorer residents of the city, who bathe and wash their clothes in it. Apart from human ashes, many dead animals end up in the Ganges, as well as wastewater from the city and ordinary rubbish. Unfortunately, the goddess Ganga urgently needs help – the Ganges is currently one of the five most polluted rivers in the world (see p. 182).

Christianity

Of the world's major religions, Christianity probably has the fewest rules about hygiene. The New Testament says almost nothing about keeping clean. It also suggests that Jesus was not strict about following Jewish cleansing customs. In fact, he criticised people who were too concerned with rituals and outward actions, and said it was best to focus on the soul. Most Christians have only one ritual bath in their entire life – their baptism.

However, Christians from the Orthodox church take annual baths to commemorate Jesus' baptism. On the night before Jesus' baptism, which falls on 19 January in the Orthodox church, believers take a dip in specially made cross-shaped baths or pools in order to cleanse themselves of sin. According to tradition, they should make the sign of the cross three times and then dip themselves in the icy holy water three times. As they step into the bath, they cry 'Christ was baptised!' and everyone else replies 'In the river Jordan!'

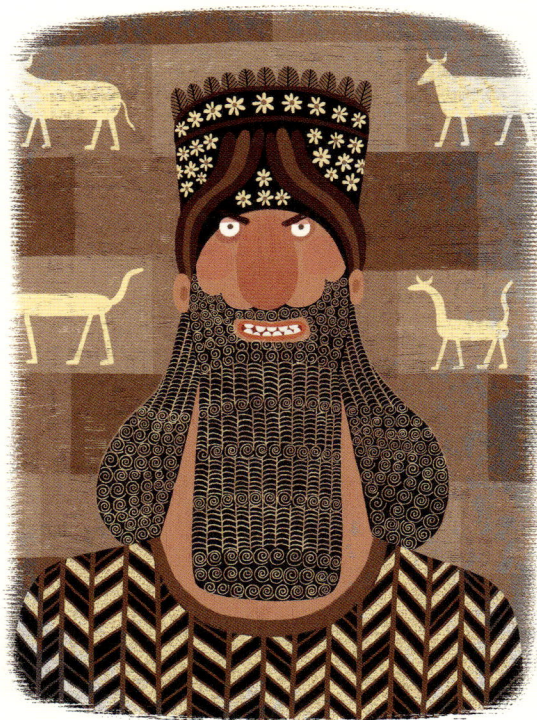

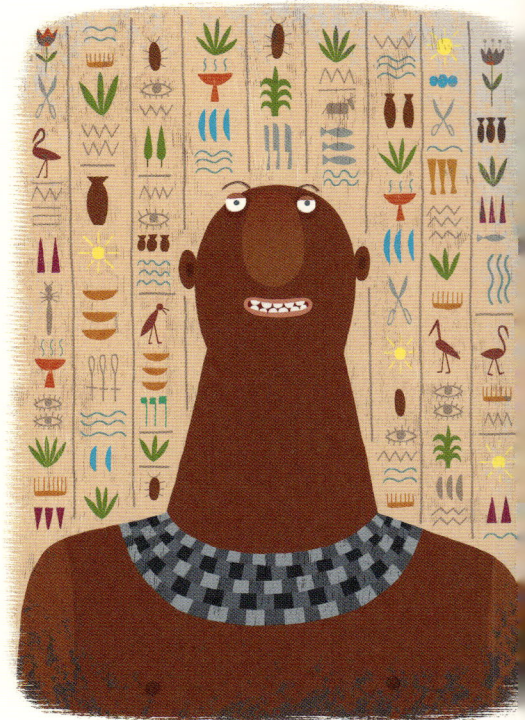

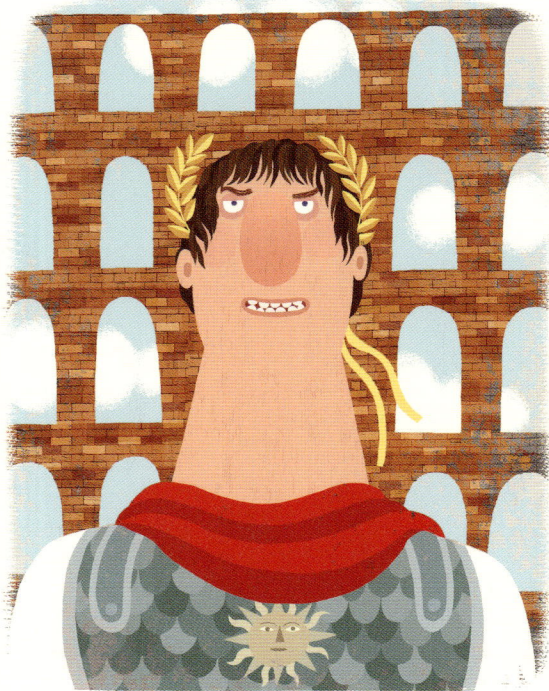

Shaved and shorn

Nowadays, an important part of keeping clean is washing and cutting your hair and shaving your legs, armpits or face. But different periods of history and different places in the world have different traditions for dealing with body hair.

The ancient Egyptians (see p. 21) removed most of the hair on their bodies. This was mostly a way to protect against skin diseases, lice and other parasites, but it was also done as a way to keep cool. The Egyptians also believed that too much hair was unhygienic and uncivilized. Hair was shaved, removed with tweezers or pumice stones, or waxed with sugar, beeswax or special creams. Men also shaved their heads, while priests even removed their eyebrows and eyelashes.

The people of ancient Persia, Greece and Rome – both men and women – usually got rid of the hair on their arms and legs. Hair was plucked out with tweezers during a visit to the baths – which is why when Seneca describes the noises coming from inside them, he mentions the yelps of people having their armpit hair removed (see p. 31). Pastes made from resins and pitch were also used to remove hair, as were roast leeches in vinegar! Many Greek and Roman women also removed their pubic hair.

For centuries, women in the Middle East removed their body hair – we know this from the accounts of the Crusaders (see

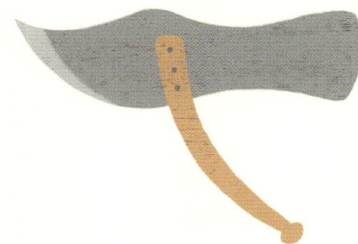

Leg-shaving became popular with women a little later in the 20th century, when dresses became shorter and shorter. But it took time for things to change. In the 1920s, an American student who cut herself while shaving her legs made newspaper headlines. It was only in the late 20th century that removing hair from legs and underarms become something that many European and American women took for granted.

However, the late 20th century also saw the start of the body positivity movement, which fights against the idea of putting pressure on people to look a certain way. Body-positive activists believe that everyone is beautiful, no matter what they look like, and promote the idea that leg and armpit hair is natural and not ugly.

p. 43) – and they still do this today. European women, meanwhile, ignored their body hair, which was hidden under their long dresses, and focused on the visible parts of their bodies. For instance, in the 16th century, rich women shaped their eyebrows and removed hair from their hairlines using a mixture that contained arsenic (see p. 95). Queen Elizabeth I was one of those who used it.

Fashion brought further changes. In 1915, an advertisement was printed in the American magazine *Harper's Bazaar*, showing a woman in a sleeveless dress waving her arms in the air, revealing her smoothly shaven armpits. The printed text said 'Summer Dress and Modern Dancing combine to make necessary the removal of objectionable hair.'

Facial hair also has a stormy history. For many centuries, it was a symbol of masculinity. The ancient Sumerians, Persians and Greeks grew long beards that they looked after carefully, sometimes even dyeing them or curling them with rollers. In ancient Egypt, some men would wear thin moustaches, but in around 1800 BCE, this was officially banned by the pharaoh. From then on, his subjects had to be clean-shaven. On special occasions, some men would wear a fake beard made of gold or other metals. Only the royal family and high-ranking priests were allowed to do this, and royal women sometimes wore them too.

In Europe, Alexander the Great was the first to make his men shave off their beards. The Greek author Plutarch writes that this happened in the year 331 BCE, on the day before a major battle with the Persians. The Persian army outnumbered the Macedonians by five to one, so Alexander, as the leader of the Macedonians, decided to make a sacrifice to Phobos, the god of fear. During their discussions, his generals asked him what else they could do. 'Shave off your beards,' said Alexander. When one of the surprised generals asked him why, he explained: 'Don't you know there's nothing more effective in a fight than grabbing the enemy by the beard?' According to some modern historians, what mattered most was that Alexander also shaved. That way, when the soldiers shaved off their facial hair, they looked more like him. This supposedly made them feel more like a team and set them apart from their bearded opponents.

Ancient Roman men also preferred smooth faces. When you look at busts of

Julius Caesar, Augustus, Marcus Agrippa, Trajan and Nero, you'll see that all of them are clean shaven. The first Roman emperor to have a beard was Hadrian in the 2nd century CE – apparently he grew it to hide a scar.

In the Enlightenment, facial hair fell out of fashion again. At the court of Louis XIV (17th century; see also p. 79), men did not even wear moustaches. Tsar Peter the Great, who admired the customs of western Europe, issued a decree in 1705 ordering Russian men to remove their beards. Those who refused had to pay a tax, and there were even cases of forced shaving.

But it was quite rare to shave heads. Japanese samurai from the Edo period (17th–19th century) did remove some of the hair from the top of their heads, but left the rest long and tied it into a ponytail at the back. Ancient Egyptians shaved their entire head but instead of leaving it bald, they wore wigs – unless they were priests. Nowadays, some Orthodox Jewish women shave their heads or cut their hair short after they get married. Tradition also requires them to cover their hair, so either they wear a headscarf – similar to the hijab worn by many Muslim women – or choose to wear a wig instead.

In Europe, wigs became popular in the 16th century because of a syphilis epidemic (see p. 95). One of the symptoms of syphilis is hair loss, so baldness was associated with the illness and became embarrassing. But the biggest craze for wigs started under Louis XIV in the 17th century (see p. 88).

Dirt and the Black Death

The Middle Ages in Europe weren't as dirty as you might think. Ordinary people would regularly go to public bath houses (see p. 44). But since women and men would often wash there together, in the late 15th and early 16th century, some people got angry and said that bathing encouraged sin. However, a much bigger threat to Europe was about to arrive – the bubonic plague. It was known as the Black Death because of the dark pus-filled lumps that appeared under patients' arms and around the groin and neck.

In 1347, rats with plague-carrying fleas arrived in Italy – and one of the biggest and most awful epidemics in the history of the world began. The Black Death was almost always fatal and it spread very fast. From Italy it soon reached Spain and France, and then continued north. It killed so many people that Europe was in chaos. People abandoned their sick relatives, leaving them to die in the street, prisoners were released

from jails because there was nobody to guard them, and there was no hope of having a proper funeral – corpses were thrown into mass graves, and when there was no more space in the cemeteries, sometimes they were even thrown into rivers.

Many terrified people believed that the plague was God's punishment for their sins. Some walked around towns whipping themselves as a form of punishment, while others decided it was too late to do anything about it and started sinning more than ever before. But there were also 'scientific' explanations. In 1348, French scholars declared that the plague was caused by the position of the planets. This was drawing 'miasma', or poisoned air, from the earth, and it was this miasma that was causing the sickness. They believed that overweight people, heavy drinkers and adulterers were most at risk from the disease, but they also thought that taking hot baths could be dangerous. These

scholars thought that warm water caused the pores of the skin to open, allowing the plague to enter the body. People began to believe bathing was a bad idea, and the public bath houses were gradually closed.

In Italy and France, doctors visiting plague victims wore a special mask with a long nose in an attempt to protect themselves. They put herbs and aromatic oils inside the nose of the mask; these were meant to block bad smells and stop them from breathing in poisoned air. Their outfit was topped off with a long coat, boots, a hat and a stick for examining patients.

These plague doctors treated the sick with magic amulets and gave them medicines made from fish scales, toad hearts, goat liver or rhinoceros horn (at least that's what they claimed – but it was probably the tusk of a narwhal, a type of dolphin). They often also recommended eating cabbages or citrus fruit, gave patients enemas, bled them or

applied frogs and leeches to the pus-filled bruises. None of these treatments did any good, just as the bird mask did nothing to prevent infection.

Now we know that the plague is caused by bacteria transferred from rats to humans by fleas, and that it can only be cured with antibiotics. Not washing makes it worse, because it means that the disease spreads faster. In four years, the Black Death killed 25 million people, which was one third of the population of Europe. And unfortunately, that wasn't the end of it – the plague returned several times over the centuries that followed.

The fear of bathing remained common in Europe for a long time. For the next three hundred and fifty years, everybody avoided water if they could. In 1538, the Dutch thinker Erasmus of Rotterdam wrote with regret that the plague had trained Europeans to live without bath houses. Even thirty years later, French doctor Ambroise Paré was repeating the idea that the body is softened by warm water and open pores let in infected air. In the mid-17th century, another French doctor, Théophraste Renaudot, claimed that bathing damages the nerves, loosens tendons and 'fills the head with vapours'.

Fortunately, our understanding of science has changed a lot since then. When the COVID-19 pandemic broke out around the world in 2019 and 2020 (a pandemic is an epidemic that happens on a much bigger scale), hygiene quickly became one of the most widespread ways of protecting ourselves. Because the COVID-19 virus was completely new, at first nobody knew how to treat the illness it causes, and we had to wait for new vaccines to be developed. That's why it was so important to keep our distance from one another, to wear face masks over our noses and mouths, and to wash and sanitize our hands regularly.

It's not only the plague and COVID-19 that can cause epidemics. In the early 20th century, Spanish flu raged across the world, killing millions of people. Meanwhile, in the early 21st century, we've already seen the SARS epidemic, bird flu, swine flu, and the Ebola epidemic that struck Africa between 2013 and 2016.

Above: The plague doesn't care who catches it. During the Black Death, a kind of popular illustration called a *danse macabre* showed people from different social classes dancing with skeletons. This reminded everyone that we are all equal in the face of death.

The Sun King's secrets

The Palace of Versailles, near Paris, is one of the most beautiful buildings of the baroque period (see p. 93). Once the home of the French kings, it was built in the late 17th century on the orders of Louis XIV, who was known as the Sun King. The cost of building and maintaining it was estimated at one quarter of the national budget. The formal rooms of the palace are huge and splendid. They include the Hall of Mirrors, where light shines in from seventeen huge windows and reflects off seventeen equally large mirrors, glittering on crystal chandeliers. However, the beauty of Versailles was only skin deep.

The rooms for servants and less important courtiers were small, dark and stuffy. But that's only the start of it. Imagine seven hundred rooms, ten thousand people, and no toilets at all! That's right, the Sun King's palace did not have a plumbing system. Instead of toilets, people used chamber pots, which were sometimes placed inside

a commode, a piece of a furniture that looked like a chair with a hole in the seat (see p. 112). But there were fewer than three hundred of these commodes in the whole palace, so not all of its residents were able to use them.

The chamber pots were emptied by servants. In theory, they were supposed to throw the contents into special cesspits, but not everyone could be bothered to walk that far, so they often poured them out of the window, splattering window sills and pavements. There were around thirty cesspits in Versailles but they weren't emptied very often because it was expensive and dangerous. The workers hired to do the job often drowned or were poisoned by gases.

Worse still, the people of Versailles who didn't have chamber pots just relieved themselves wherever they liked. Sometimes this meant behind a bush in the garden, which was no big deal. However, it was quite common for people to pee and poo anywhere inside the palace – in the corners of rooms, behind the curtains, in corridors and on the stairs. People would shout 'The king is coming!' as a warning, whenever Louis was on his way. The problem was not solved until 1715, shortly before Louis died, when there was an order that waste should be removed from Versailles – but only once a week. Some people claim that even though the palace has been cleaned and refurbished many times since the reign

of the Sun King, the furthest nooks and crannies still smell like pee.

As well as thousands of people, lots of animals also lived in the royal palace. Many courtiers kept dogs in their chambers, and nobody cleaned up after them. Cows and goats were often brought inside too, to provide ladies with fresh, warm milk. The beds were full of bugs and fleas, and mice and rats nested behind the carved wooden panels. Rats were very common in Versailles because the palace cooks weren't too bothered about hygiene and left bits of food scattered all over the kitchens.

A house says a lot about the people who live in it. The Sun King, like his father (who first took a bath at the age of seven) and his grandfather, simply stank. The stench was so bad that the ladies of the court would sniff perfumed handkerchiefs whenever he was around so that they didn't faint. The situation was made worse by the fact that Louis XIV loved sport. That might be healthy, but instead of washing

after exercise, he'd only change his shirt (see p. 87).

And the king was not the only smelly one – his servants and courtiers were slobs, as were the ladies-in-waiting who complained about the royal pong. At that time, many Europeans believed bathing was dangerous (see p. 76). Sometimes they would wash their hands and faces, but not very well. Even the king's morning routine involved very little water. Louis would rinse his mouth out, quickly dip his hands in alcohol or perfume and wipe his face with a damp cloth.

A proper bath was recommended very rarely by doctors – only if other medical treatments, such as blood-letting, hadn't worked. Louis's doctors once prescribed a bath to boost his strength after an illness. Before it, they took various precautions, including giving the king an enema and making him rest. But it wasn't enough – the 'dangerous' bath caused a terrible migraine.

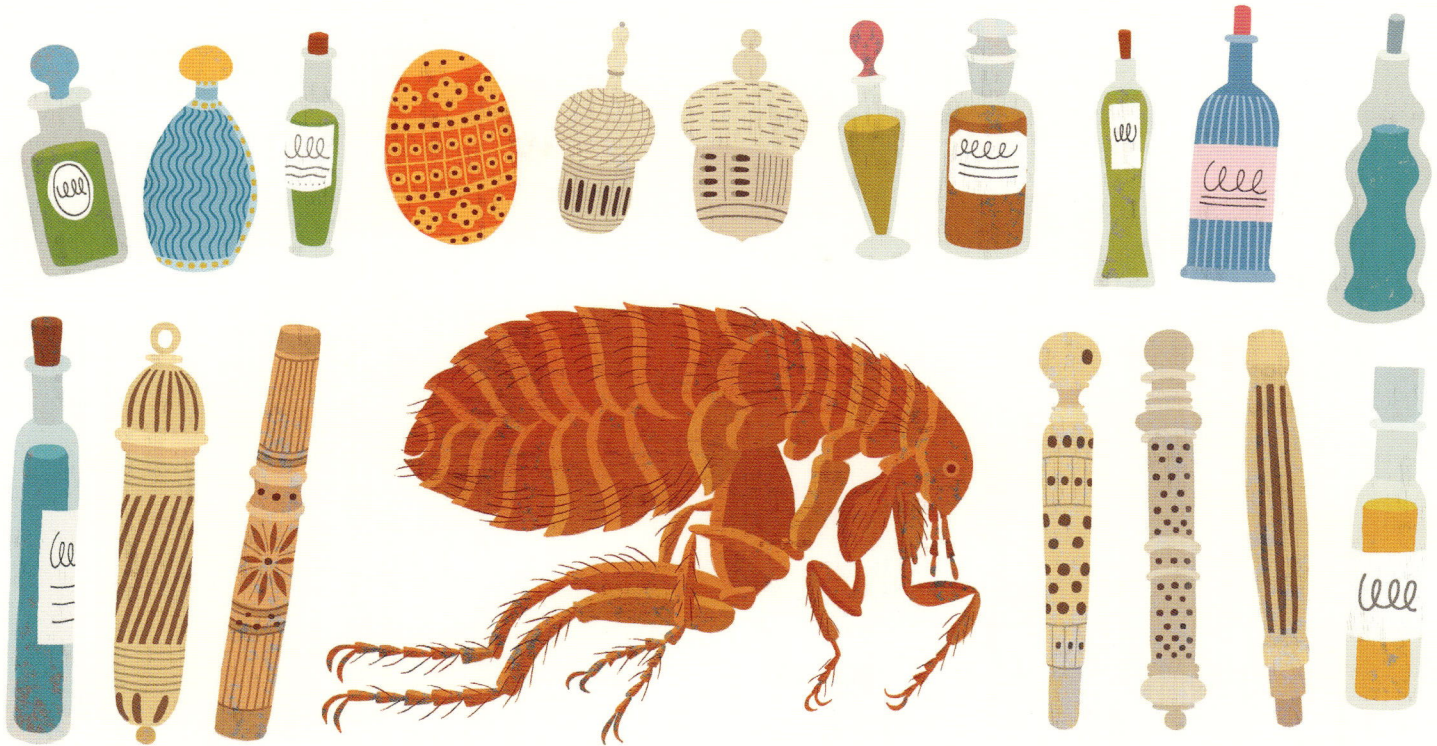

Clean shirts and a wig full of mice

Although in the Renaissance and the Enlightenment (16th–18th centuries), Europeans were afraid of water and would at most dabble their fingertips in it (see p. 74), they'd be very shocked if someone were to call them filthy. They were wearing clean shirts, after all!

At that time, shirts were considered under-wear – they were worn over bare skin. People thought that fabric had cleansing properties. They believed sweat was made of the same substances as manure, so linen yarn, which was made from plant fibres, absorbed it best. It was believed to be an excellent way to clean the skin – and much safer than a bath! It was also said that people of the ancient world used to wash so often (see p. 29) because they didn't wear shirts, and that was because they didn't know about their wonderful properties.

Renaissance and Enlightenment shirts were white and they were always washed very thoroughly. The richest people owned many spares and changed them as soon as they became dirty. Louis XIV (see p. 79) was such a stickler for cleanliness that he changed his shirt several times a day

– even though he never bathed his body underneath.

In the Middle Ages, underwear was usually hidden beneath outer layers of clothing. Once it began to be seen as a symbol of cleanliness, people were much bolder and keener to show it off. That's probably why over time, it became increasingly fancy, with lace trims, flounced sleeves and frills.

Rich people also found an alternative for washing their hair – wearing wigs. At first, wealthy Europeans wore wigs to hide the fact that they were going bald (see p. 70), but when Louis XIV also began losing his hair and started to wear one, wigs quickly became a symbol of power and high social class. Other kings copied Louis's wig, soon followed by their courtiers and aristocrats.

At first, the new fashion really did make it easier to stay clean – because unlike a head, you could boil a wig in water and kill any bugs in it.

Over time, however, wigs became much bigger and fancier. By the late 18th century, they were giant structures made of a mixture of real and fake hair, built on special frames and richly decorated with ribbons, lace, feathers, beads, precious stones, fake flowers, fruit and even small ornaments. Known as *poufs*, these huge hairpieces could weigh almost a kilogram and were dizzyingly high. They also couldn't easily be taken off because people's real hair was woven into them. Some wig-wearers couldn't walk down corridors with low ceilings. They had to sleep sitting up, and when they rode in

carriages, they had to stick their heads out of the window.

Since it took a great deal of time and money to make these wigs, ladies rarely brushed them out. In 1768, the *London Magazine* wrote a sarcastic article about a woman who had dismantled her hairstyle after just nine weeks! No wonder these wigs were teeming with fleas and lice, and sometimes larger creatures – if a wig was left in a wardrobe, mice could easily make a nest in it.

But fashionable folk fought back. Instead of dealing with the cause of the problem, by giving up wigs and washing their hair,

they invented tools for fighting the bugs. To provide relief from itchy skin, they used special scratchers with long handles, often made from expensive materials and decorated with beautiful carvings. Nobody was surprised to see a gentleman or lady of the court sticking this kind of gadget into their hair and scratching vigorously. What's more, they put tiny lice-traps – carved ivory boxes containing bundles of wool soaked in blood or honey – inside wigs, and killed any creepy-crawlies they caught with special gold or silver hammers. Head lice are still common today, but we now use special shampoo and combs to get rid of them.

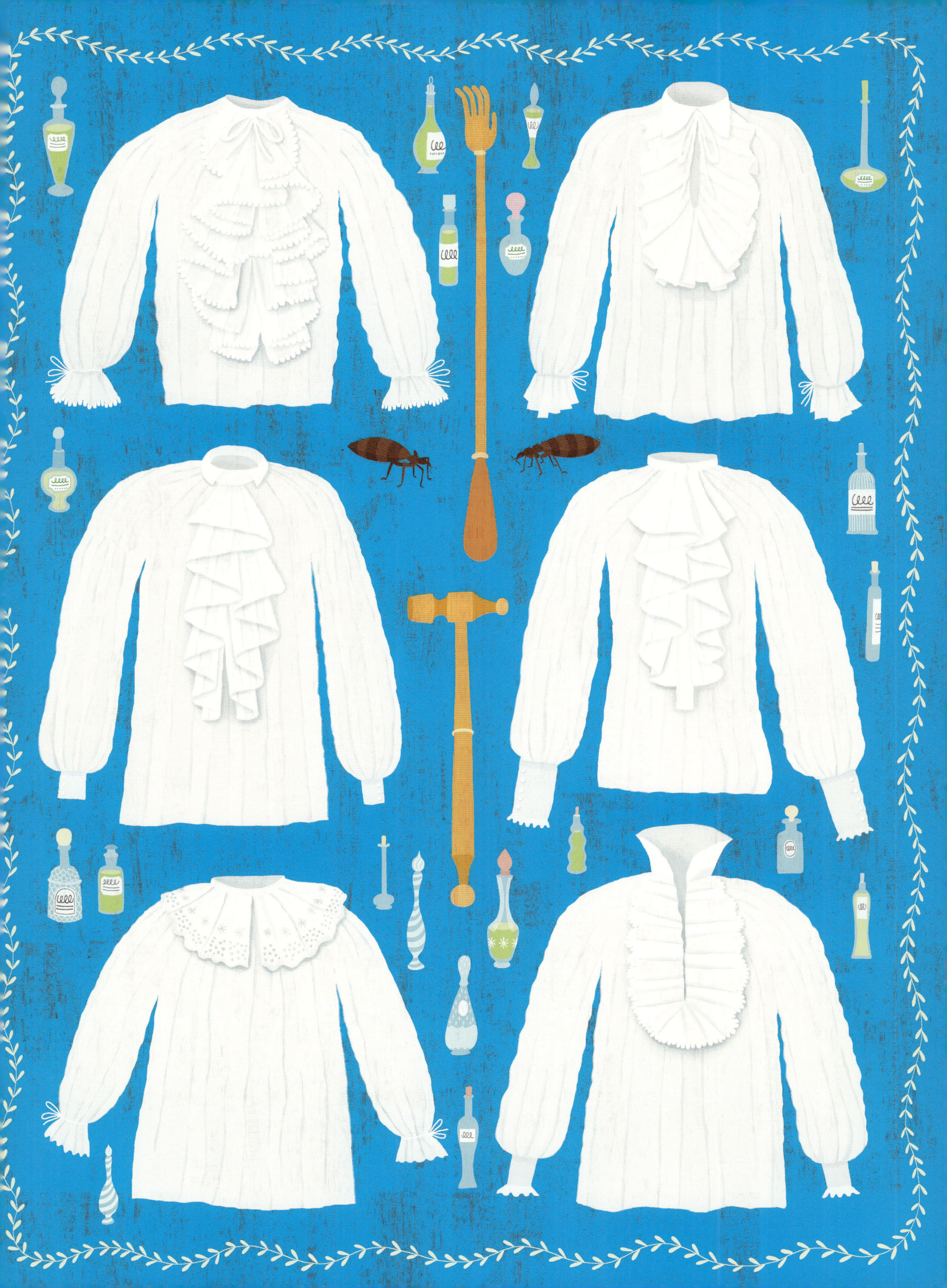

Poisonous powders

Baroque paintings often show men and women with porcelain-white faces, bright red lips and flushed pink cheeks. The baroque period (17th–18th centuries) was a very theatrical time in art, when strange and exotic things were admired. Paintings from the period often featured optical illusions, while in architecture everything was covered in decorations and ornaments, which meant things often looked fancy and fake. This was also true in fashion. Striking make-up, intricate wigs and luxurious costumes were mostly just a way to hide dirt, smells and diseases.

Pale skin had been admired in Europe since ancient times – it was seen as a sign of health and high standing. Tanned skin, which is now considered attractive, used to be linked with working outdoors and therefore with the lower social classes. If someone had pale skin, it showed that they could afford to laze around at home or in their palace. Since ancient times, people had tried to achieve that look by painting on toxic white lead (see p. 24).

A thick layer of white make-up also helped hide skin imperfections. In the 17th and 18th centuries, apart from bubonic plague, smallpox was also widespread. Those who survived it were left with deep scars known as pockmarks. A lover of the Polish king Stanisław August was said to be

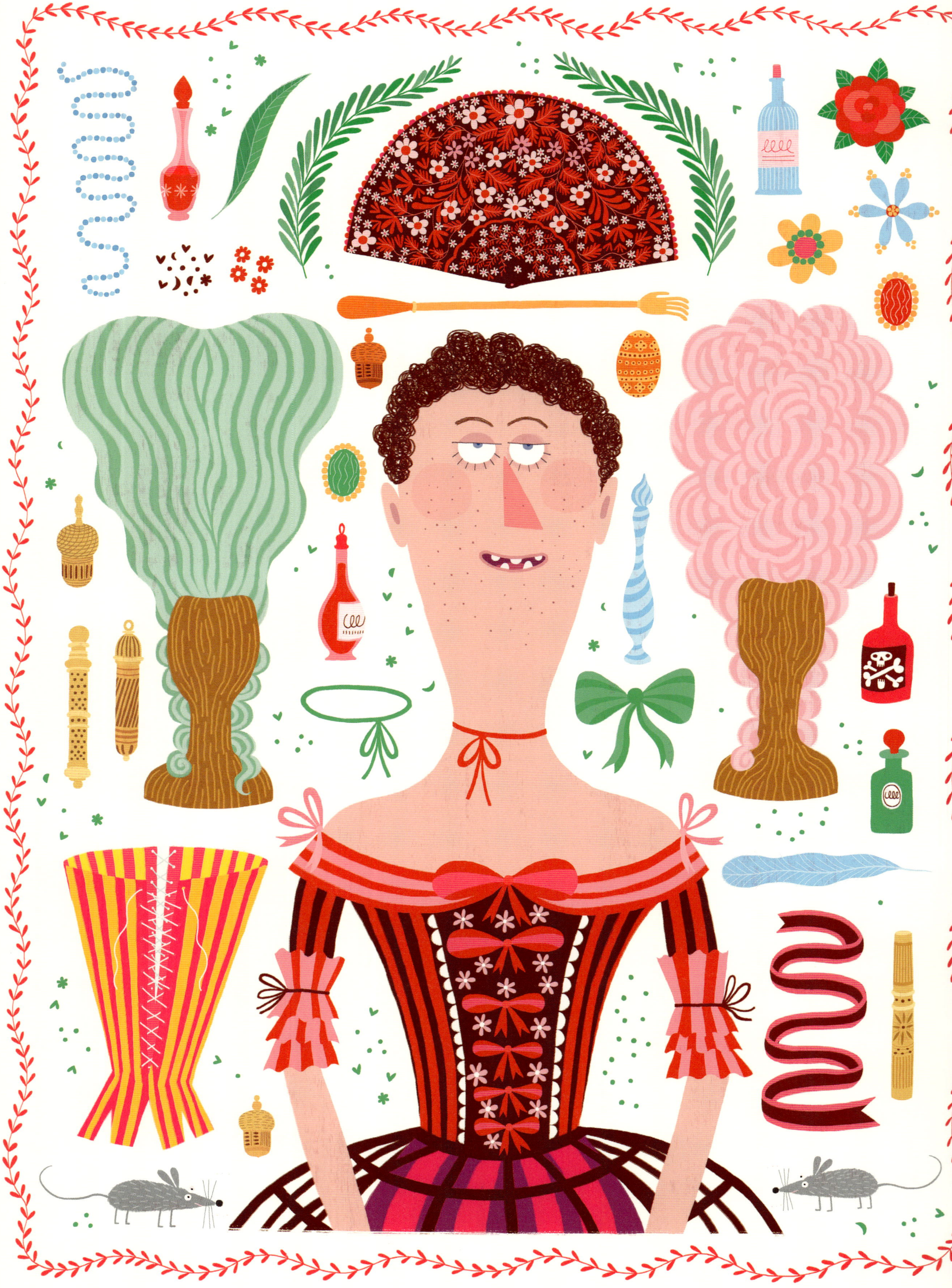

'so pockmarked, as if devils had thrashed her face with peas'. Another common disease at the time was syphilis (see p. 70), which caused stains and ulcers on the skin.

The lead used in make-up made the skin turn grey and sallow, or even yellow, green or blue. It also blocked the skin's pores which meant the skin couldn't 'breathe'. Even worse, the lead got into the blood stream and poisoned the whole body. As a result, fashionable ladies would find that their hair fell out and their teeth rotted. Sometimes it even poisoned their lungs and caused mental illness.

And that's not all. Other popular skin-lightening products contained the poison arsenic, which could cause kidney disease, blindness, bleeding, baldness and diseases of the skin and nervous system. If it was used for a long time, it could even be deadly (see p. 68).

After applying whitener, women would put rouge on their cheeks. The dye used in this contained cinnabar, another name for mercury sulphide. You guessed it – that was poisonous, too. The mercury also caused discoloured and peeling skin. And the only way to hide the effects of this toxic make-up was to wear more and more.

Any spots, ulcers or scars that couldn't be hidden with make-up were papered over with fake beauty spots, also called 'mouches'. These were made of black silk, taffeta or leather. They were usually round, but sometimes came in fancier shapes such as stars, moons, hearts or animals. One British princess apparently wore a beauty patch in the shape of a horse-drawn carriage.

The whole look was finished off with darkened eyebrows (created with a mixture made from burnt almonds), bright red lips and a thick layer of rice or cereal

powder. Wigs were also heavily powdered (see p. 88) – usually they were a shade of light grey, but sometimes the powder was dyed blue, purple, pink or yellow. Powdered wigs became so common that by the end of the 18th century, the British government put a tax on them in order to gather money for the war with France.

Nowadays, we use perfume to show how elegant, well-groomed and clean we are. In the past, however, people used it to cover their own smell and to hide the stink of others. For instance, one of the mistresses of French king Louis XIV (see p. 79) would dab on plenty of perfume before meeting with him in order to mask the smell of his bad breath.

People tried to cover the smell of greasy hair and dirty wigs by dusting their hair with power scented with lavender, orris root and orange flower. The scent of unwashed bodies and dirty clothes was also hidden with flowery eau de toilette and strong perfumes containing ingredients such as civet, ambergris and musk. These names may sound quite innocent, but do you know where these substances come from? Civet and musk come from glands near the bottoms of civets and musk deer, while ambergris is a waxy substance that is made inside the guts of sperm whales. What's more, these ingredients are still used in some perfumes today.

As well as these perfumes, people applied creams made of resins and plant oils. Some of these smelled so strong that they could make sensitive souls feel dizzy and ill. In case that wasn't enough, they wore pomanders under their clothes – these were small gold, silver or crystal cases filled with perfumes.

The Great Stink

Modern towns are not always clean. Sometimes there is dog poo or litter in the streets, many places are fighting a constant battle against smog, and the rivers flowing through others are often in a grimy state. But that's nothing compared to what they were like in the past!

Throughout history, one of the biggest problems for European towns was the lack of sewers. People had to poo and pee outdoors in a simple toilet called a privy or outhouse, or indoors in a chamber pot (see p. 112). Children often did their business on streets and in doorways because they were afraid of the privies. No wonder – if the board beneath you snapped, which did sometimes happen, you might fall into a deep pit of poo and drown.

The contents of chamber pots were supposed to be thrown into the privies, but often they were poured out of the window onto

the street, along with dirty dishwater. In Edinburgh, people would yell 'Gardyloo!' as they emptied the pot, to warn people passing by underneath. The word came from the French *garde à l'eau*, which means 'watch out for the water'! To make things easier, some towns set special hours for emptying chamber pots.

Nasty experiences could happen to anyone. The writer Jan Długosz recorded how King Władysław Jagiełło of Poland (14th–15th century) had dishwater thrown over him during a trip to Toruń when he came to visit the Grand Master of the Teutonic Order of Knights. Apparently, the Grand Master wanted to have the cook who had thrown the water put to death, but the king asked him to spare her life.

A slightly better solution was to empty chamber pots into the river. In medieval London, there were several public toilets on London Bridge, so the waste dropped straight into the Thames, but not all of it was washed away.

As well as human waste, rubbish and left-over food would also be thrown out of the

windows of medieval homes, providing a feast for rats and other animals.

Open channels called gutters ran along the side of the streets and acted as a sewage system. Everything that was thrown out of windows landed in them, as well as waste from dyeworks, papermills, breweries and tanneries, and sometimes even animal guts. In 14th-century London, meat merchants threw their leftovers straight into the Thames from a riverbank known as Bochersbrigge or 'Butchers' Bridge'. The gutters were not only incredibly smelly, they were also very dangerous. Some were so deep that drunk people or small children could drown in them.

Anything that didn't end up in the gutters usually stayed where it was. As a result, the level of the ground grew gradually higher. In the Middle Ages, the streets of many old European cities were sometimes several metres lower than they are today!

Anything that did end up in the gutters flowed into the river. You can probably imagine how unpleasant this was. In the middle of the 19th century, the British

scientist Michael Faraday wrote that in London, the surface of the Thames was so filthy that you could see the greasy clouds of sewage even through its murky brown water. This had terrible consequences for the people who lived nearby.

In 1854, John Snow, a doctor in London who was studying victims of cholera, a deadly disease, realized that the cause of the illness was polluted water. He hit upon this idea when he noticed that the only people who had not fallen sick were brewery workers, because they only drank beer. Unfortunately, nobody believed him. Back then, most people thought diseases were caused by poisoned air (see p. 74).

But four years later, during a summer heatwave, the water level in the Thames dropped so low that the tonnes of sewage lying at the bottom could be seen. The city was filled with such a horrible stench that even the politicians in the Houses of Parliament, which stands on the riverbank, complained. It was only after this disaster, which is known as the Great Stink, that a proper sewer system was built in London.

Churches also gave off a terrible pong in those days. Dead bodies were laid to rest in vaults and graveyards that were so full, the graves would often cave in and the stench of corpses would waft out. The idea of burying the dead outside town is relatively new. In

France, it was Louis XVI (18th century) who banned burials inside churches and around them. That was when one of the biggest graveyards in Paris was cleared – the Holy Innocents' Cemetery. In the space of two years, around twenty thousand bodies were dug out from a layer of graves that was ten metres deep.

Modern cities have problems with traffic fumes, but in the past it was horse manure that caused trouble, because horses were the main form of public transport. As cities grew, the number of horses increased and people couldn't clean up the manure quickly enough. In the late 19th century, the *Times* newspaper predicted that by 1950, if things

carried on in the same way, the streets of London would be covered in three metres of dung. In New York, horse manure was expected to reach the second floor of homes by 1930. That's not surprising when you find out that 150,000 horses worked in Manhattan at the time. Each horse produced twelve kilograms of poo per day, which in total made over 1,500 tonnes of manure every 24 hours. When a lady or gentleman wanted to cross the street, special workers would shovel a path through the dung. It was also gathered into heaps, which attracted swarms of flies. Doctors estimated that 20,000 people died in New York every year from diseases spread this way.

In the throne room

The toilet is one of the oldest human inventions. Interestingly, it was invented several times, in different periods and places across the world.

Five thousand years ago, the Egyptians used stone or wooden seats with an opening above a bowl for catching waste – but this was a luxury only the richest people could afford. Five hundred years later, in the town of Mohenjo Daro on the Indus river (in modern-day Pakistan), almost everybody had toilets in their homes. No traces of a palace or temples have been found in the ruins of that ancient metropolis, but the city did boast seven hundred wells and a huge public swimming pool or water tank, which historians now call the 'Great Bath'. And, most remarkably of all, it had a sewage network that even included the toilets in private houses: the toilets were stone benches with

holes in them, flushed with water brought from the wells.

This level of hygiene was not matched until 1,500 years later, by the Romans in around 800 BCE (see p. 41). The wealthiest people had homes connected to the sewers and toilets that they flushed using water from a bucket. Toilets were usually located in the kitchen. This allowed them to throw their cooking waste into the drains, too. Everybody else paid a small fee to use public toilets, which were also connected to the sewage network, but they were completely different to the ones we know today. In a Roman public toilet, you did your business in company, sitting in a row on a long stone bench with holes in it. Nobody was embarrassed about this – in fact, they'd often sit around, making jokes or talking about politics. Some historians even think that at least a few of these places were open to both men and women.

Matters were much worse in medieval towns, which didn't have sewers (see p. 99). People relieved themselves in privies or outhouses, a small shed built on top of a cesspit that could be up to five metres deep. These pits were often leaky, so some of

the waste would spread into nearby wells. When a pit became full, it was covered in earth and the outhouse on top was moved to another spot. In later years, cesspits were emptied by workers called 'nightmen' or 'gong farmers', because 'gong' was a word for manure. The waste was taken away to fields and rivers, or simply thrown over the city walls.

Outhouses are still used in many places around the world. The modern-day Portaloo is basically the same kind of thing. In the Polish countryside in the 1920s, people used to do their business in fields, gardens or pigsties. Out of concern for citizens' health and hygiene, the politician Felicjan Sławoj Składkowski made it the law that every Polish home had to have an outhouse. Then he travelled the country to see for himself whether people were obeying the rule!

In medieval castles, the toilets were built in special towers or small rooms that stuck out from the castle wall. That way, waste dropped straight into the moat underneath. You can see this kind of structure in many Crusader castles, and also in the Wawel Castle in the centre of Kraków, Poland. One of its towers still houses a small room

that contains a stone slab with a hole in it, covered by a wooden board. Below the hole is a long shaft, 8 metres deep.

Chamber pots were also used in the ancient world (see p. 41). The Romans used copper ones, while richer people owned pots of silver or gold. Later, earthenware pots were used, and eventually porcelain ones – sometimes they were so beautifully decorated, you might mistake them for a soup dish. One type of chamber pot was a narrow oval-shaped design called a 'bourdaloue'. This was named after a 12th-century priest called Louis Bourdaloue, who preached at the Palace of Versailles (see p. 79). His sermons were popular but also very long, so women began to take gravy boats to chapel so they could discreetly have a pee during mass. Dutch pottery factories quickly copied this idea and began making chamber pots in the same boat-like shape.

Towards the end of the Middle Ages, it became more common for wealthy homes to have a toilet. It usually took the form of a box or chair with a hole in the seat and a chamber pot or bucket underneath. These toilets were often lavishly decorated! The Italian princess Beatrice d'Este is said to have owned a commode designed by Leonardo da Vinci (15th–16th century). It had a silver seat with a carved handrail, a woven silk canopy and a gold pot underneath. Beatrice's husband asked Leonardo for a music box to go with it, but the artist

refused, saying he was too busy working on *The Last Supper*.

For a long time, historians believed that the flushing toilet was invented in the late 16th century by the English poet John Harington, godson of Queen Elizabeth 1. The queen had one installed in one of her palaces, but nobody else followed suit. It was an expensive and complicated contraption and bad smells would waft out of the toilet bowl.

In the 18th century, the idea came back into fashion. A breakthrough came in 1775, when the Scottish clockmaker Alexander Cumming had the brilliant idea of fitting a pipe with a bend underneath the bowl, in the shape of a sideways 'S'. The water that was left behind in the bend after flushing meant the smell didn't escape. There still weren't any sewage pipes, however, so the waste was emptied into cesspits, gutters or rivers. Proper sewers were first built in European towns in the second half of the 19th century (see p. 103).

But the British were by no means the first users of water closets or WCs. In 2000, archaeologists discovered a flushing toilet in the tomb of Liu Wu, a prince of the Western

Han dynasty, from over 2,000 years ago. This splendid stone commode was almost as comfortable as modern ones; it could be flushed out with jugs of water and it even had armrests. Another ancient toilet was found in the 3000-year-old ruins of the royal palace in Crete.

A very special servant

There's one place that even kings had to go on foot, rather than in a carriage or on a horse – the toilet. But unlike the rest of us, they often didn't go there alone. Many of them did their business in the presence of courtiers and some wouldn't even interrupt their royal duties while doing so – they'd continue negotiations or discussions with their subjects while they relieved themselves.

King Władysław Jagiełło of Poland (14th–15th century; see pp. 100 and 157), for instance, held audiences on the loo. The writer Jan Długosz recorded that after a meal, the 'stuffed [King] fell into a deep, long sleep, after which he left his bed for a secluded place and for a long time passed stools, while getting much work done. He

was apparently never more approachable or gentle than at this time. Knights would try to catch him in these moments because it was easier to make him agree to what they were asking.'

Meanwhile, British kings in the 15th and 16th centuries were always accompanied by a special servant, called the 'groom of the

stool'. The name came from the term for the royal commode (stool). The man with this job looked after the king's most private tasks: making his bed, dressing him, washing him – and yes, helping the monarch to use the toilet.

How did this work? In a special curtained room, there was a box padded with crimson velvet. Under its lid, there was a round opening and inside, a chamber pot. The groom of the stool brought the king a bowl of water and some cloths for wiping himself, helped him undress, and removed the chamber pot once it was all over. Historians don't know whether his tasks also involved wiping the royal bottom.

This might sound like the worst job a courtier could have, but in fact it was a great honour. To get the job, you had to be completely trusted by the king or have friends in high places. The groom of the stool was one of the most influential people at court, because he knew the kings's secrets and had constant access to him. Other courtiers treated him with great respect, and sometimes even feared him.

That's because his duties didn't just concern the toilet. Hugh Denys, groom of the stool to Henry VII, also looked after state taxes, while in Henry VIII's time, the title of grooms of the stool was given to a whole group of courtiers who were something like royal secretaries. Towards the end of Henry's life, one of his grooms was even allowed to use his royal seal, which meant he was very powerful.

Clearly, this job wasn't given to ordinary servants, but to noblemen from good families. After years of loyal service, many of them became highly successful and very wealthy. Hugh Denys, for instance, married an aristocrat, owned four estates and held many important government positions.

However, the habit of welcoming visitors while on the toilet could be deadly. In 1589, a young monk named Jacques Clément arrived to see the French king Henry III. He said he had a very urgent letter, so the guards took him to the king, who was on the toilet. Clément kneeled before the king and handed him the letter, and when Henry began to read it, Clément stabbed him in

the stomach with a dagger. Doctors tried to put the victim's insides back into his body and also gave him an enema, but it didn't help – the king died the following day.

When Louis XIV of France (see p. 79) was doing his business, he was usually accompanied by around a hundred people! Yes, you guessed it – seeing the Sun King on the toilet was considered an honour. Once the king had finished, clerks known as 'bearers of the chair of interests' handed him cloths to wipe himself, and then doctors studied the contents of the chamber pot before the bearers removed it.

In 1686, the king needed an operation on his bottom and this was also a public event. He was accompanied by the closest members of his family, a confessor and the prime minister, who held his hand. For some time after the event, it was fashionable at Versailles to wear bandages, and some courtiers even asked the royal surgeon to perform the same operation on them, even though they were perfectly healthy.

The 'Polish plait'

There's a strange object on show inside a glass case at the museum of the department of medicine at the Jagiellonian University of Kraków in Poland. It looks a bit like a giant dreadlock. It's 150 cm long, it's from the 19th century and it's known as a *plica polonica*.

Just a few centuries ago, many Europeans believed that baths could make people ill (see p. 76). The same was true of washing hair. Instead, doctors recommended brushing on powder and then combing it out. In the countryside, people didn't even do that. Peasants not only never washed their hair, they also didn't cut or brush it. They almost always wore hats or shawls. As a result, the hair became tangled and matted, felting into clumps mixed with sweat and dirt as well as lice and other bugs.

These thick 'plaits' of hair came in all shapes and sizes. They could be long or short, knotty or smooth, formed from a single mass or made of many clumps braided together. A single large plica was called a 'female', while one with many strands was called a 'male'. The longest ones were waist-length. They were particularly common in Poland – hence the Latin name, *plica polonica*, which means 'Polish plait'. In the 18th century, this condition affected more than half of all Polish countryfolk.

Strangely enough, nobody realized that the plica was the result of poor hygiene. Instead, people thought it was a symptom of an illness. It was believed that everybody had a plica inside them, also known as a 'guest'. The guest was harmless while it was asleep, but it was very easy to wake it up – by annoying it, for instance. So, if the plica inside you wanted a drink or didn't want to go and work in the fields, you had no choice but to obey!

The plica could also be woken by demons, spells, a nasty glance, or by getting a bat entangled in your hair. People even believed that an evil innkeeper might soak his own plica in vodka and then feed it to customers to make them sick and drunk.

Once it had woken up, a 'guest' was thought to move around inside the body, where it caused various problems – pains, breathlessness, aching bones, dizziness, weakness. Finally, it would creep into the hair and glue the individual shafts together into a plica. This was the way that the sickness left the body. The forming of a plica was therefore a welcome thing, and people even tried to speed up the process by dipping their hair in herbal extracts or rubbing various substances into it.

Once the plica was in your hair, you could remove it, and the sickness it embodied. But this couldn't be done straight away! People believed that cutting it off too soon or in the wrong way could make the 'guest' seek revenge – it could make you blind or deaf, or cause bleeding, paralysis, insanity or even death. You had to wait for the plica to fall off by itself, though there were several ways to encourage this – for instance by wrapping your head in hedgehog skin. Simply cutting it off was not an option, unless a special procedure was followed. The most sensible thing was to wait one year and six weeks, and then go to a specialist healer. You could visit the healer on an empty stomach, on a fine day, but never on a Friday, and best of all on Easter Saturday. He would cut it off, wrap it in a cloth, place a coin and a piece of bread inside the bundle, sprinkle vodka on it and bury it at the foot of a roadside cross or chapel, or take it outside the village. Plicas were usually sliced off with an axe or a sickle sprinkled with holy water, but sometimes they were set alight on the patient's head or even chewed off!

But the weirdest thing of all was that many doctors believed the plica was a genuine disease. Some even believed it was catching. Some also thought that cutting off the plica too soon could be very dangerous for the patient.

Changes occurred slowly. When in the 17th century, a doctor from Scotland who was working at the court of the Polish king John II Casimir, declared that the best treatment for plicas was water, scissors and a comb, a Polish bishop called him a Scottish donkey. Over time, however, more and more doctors started cutting off plicas with a pair of scissors. One of the more outspoken of them was Józef Dietl, a professor and politician from Kraków. In the mid-19th century, he made an official list of all plica-wearers in Galicia, an area between modern-day Poland and Ukraine, and banned them from entering some buildings. People suspected this was the first step towards a tax on plicas, so they started to cut off their plicas themselves. Of course, nobody was harmed when they did it – but for a long time, people explained this by saying they must have been fake plicas all along!

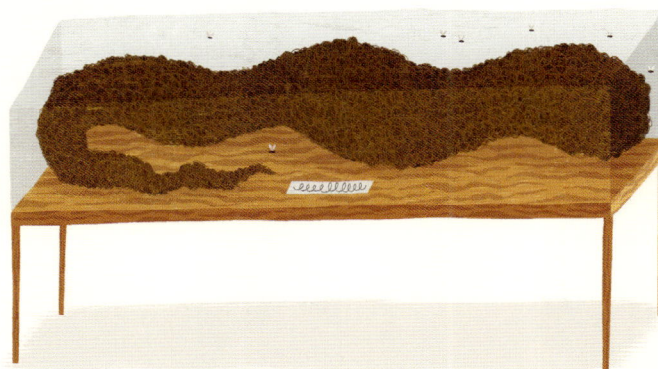

No sweat

Washing is one way to clean yourself, but sweating is another way. It has been done for hundreds of years in many places around the world. The ancient Romans sweated in their public baths (see p. 29), and the Turkish sweated in hammams (see p. 43) – and some still do today. For centuries, many people around the world, including the Japanese, Finns, Russians and Native Americans, have sweated as a way of becoming clean. Steam baths, or saunas, have many advantages. They ease tired muscles, strengthen immunity, boost blood circulation, reduce blood pressure, and unblock the pores of the skin.

Finnish saunas (dry saunas)

This is probably the best-known type of sauna. Modern Finnish saunas are usually small, wood-lined rooms, containing a stove with stones on the top. From time to time, water is poured on the stones to create steam. Finnish saunas are very dry – the air humidity is usually around 15%. They're also very hot – the temperature can reach up to 100°c! Users of the sauna are

naked. Shy people can wear a towel, but they shouldn't wear anything underneath. Once they've had enough of the heat, they take a cold shower.

In Finland, there are over one and a half million saunas, and almost all Finns regularly use them. There's even a sauna in the Finnish parliament! Modern saunas are heated with an electric stove. Traditional ones are small huts with a wood-burning stove. They are often built next to a river or lake so that people can leap straight into the water afterwards. In winter, you can also cool down in the snow.

Interestingly, in Finland long ago, saunas were the cleanest rooms in the house, so they were also used as places for women to give birth. One Finnish president was born in a sauna, and when he grew up, he also held talks with Soviet diplomats in them!

Roman baths (steam rooms)

In a Roman bath, the temperature is quite low (40–60°C), but it's very humid indeed, which is why it feels much hotter. The high level of humidity means a steam room can't be made of wood. It has to be built with ceramic tiles, plastic or stone. There is no stove but a special steam generator. A Roman bath can also be used for a herbal sauna, where herbal extracts and fragrant oils are added to the water used to create the steam.

Banya

This is the Russian version of a sauna and it's particularly popular in Siberia. Like a traditional Finnish sauna, it's a small wooden hut, often near a river or lake. Inside, there are usually three rooms: an entrance room, a steam room and a bathing room. In the

entrance room, you can get changed and drink tea or *kvass* (a drink made from fermented bread) while the sauna heats up. The steam room contains a wood-burning stove with stones on top of it. Water and herbs are poured onto the stones to create steam. The temperature reaches between 80 and 120°C, and humidity is about 60%. Every now and then, you have to take a break to cool down, either in the third room, or outside in the river, lake or snow.

During their time in the steam room, guests may also whack each other with a special brush called a bath besom or sauna whisk, which is made of birch or oak branches and leaves.

Ganbanyoku (rock sauna)

A Japanese sauna. In a ganbanyoku, you lie on volcanic rock that's heated to around 40–44°C. One session lasts between 45 minutes and an hour. After the session, you have to take a shower because the sweat produced by a rock sauna is very different to normal sweat. In Japanese it is called 'pearl' sweat. It doesn't smell, it's very thick and acts as a moisturizer for the skin. People who want to lose weight also head to the ganbanyoku – you can burn up to 1500 calories there, which is more or less the same as running for ten kilometres!

Legend has it that the ganbanyoku was invented by Japanese samurai from the island of Hokkaido. One day after a battle, they hid in the mountains. They saw a group of monkeys bathing in the hot springs, and then resting on the nearby stones. The warriors did the same thing and found that their wounds healed surprisingly fast as a result.

Sweat lodges

Some Native American nations traditionally use a sauna-like space called a sweat lodge. It's normally a kind of tent – a rounded dome covered with animal skins or blankets. Inside, under the dome, they dig a small hole, which they fill with rocks that have been heated on a fire. Water is then poured over them to create steam.

A visit to a sweat lodge is not only important for hygiene and health – it's also a religious ceremony. Sweating cleanses the body, mind and soul at the same time. Each session is run by an experienced leader who knows how to keep everyone safe. Before entering the lodge, those taking part may make a sacrifice on an altar, and inside they pray and beat drums in order to summon good spirits. It's a powerful experience – the lodge is dark and very hot inside, and the ceremony sometimes lasts several hours.

Some non-Native American people are fascinated by this ritual and try to copy it, but they don't have the knowledge that Native Americans have passed down from generation to generation. Sometimes this can have tragic consequences – at least nine people have died in fake sweat lodges, as a result of dehydration and suffocation.

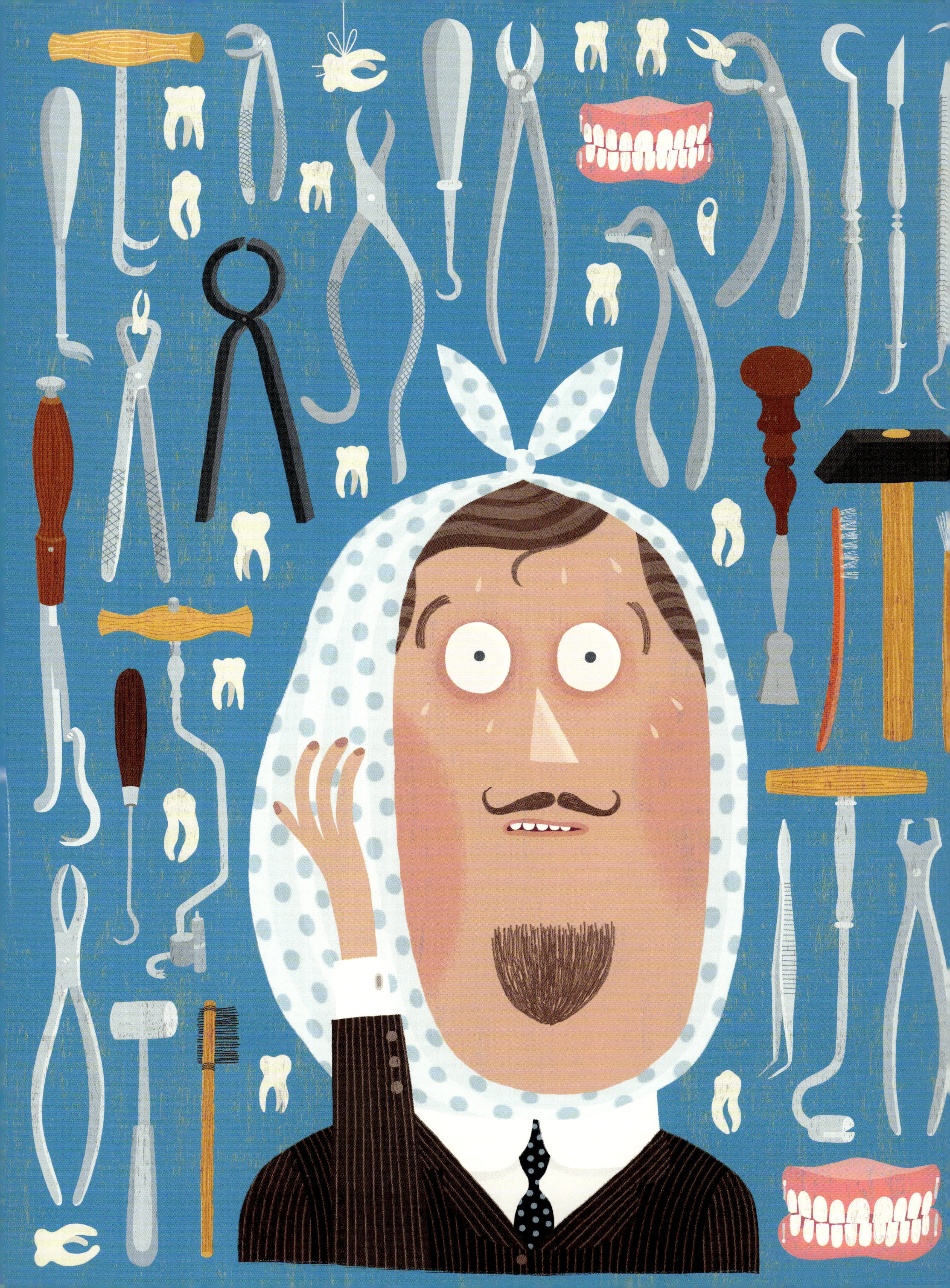

Brush hour

Did you brush your teeth this morning? Let's hope so! Inventions like the toothbrush, toothpaste and dental floss are really worth celebrating.

The earliest method for cleaning teeth was simply to pick out leftover food. Neanderthals did this 50,000 years ago, and people continued to do so for millennia, using grasses, twigs, small bones or whatever they could get their hands on. The ancient Romans apparently liked to pick their teeth with porcupine quills.

Later, people began making special tools for removing food from between their teeth. In a Viking funeral boat from the 9th century, archaeologists discovered a gold toothpick. In 16th-century England, Queen Elizabeth 1 had a toothpick decorated with rubies. The Dutch scholar Erasmus of Rotterdam (15th–16th centuries) wrote

that leftover food should be removed 'not using a knife or fingernails, in the manner of dogs or cats, nor with a napkin, but with a toothpick of mastic wood or with a feather or small bones from the drumsticks of a cockerel or hen'.

The first mass-produced toothbrush was made in Europe in the late 18th century, but brushes were first used to clean teeth 5,500 years earlier in Mesopotamia and 5,000 years ago in Egypt (see p. 21).

The earliest toothbrushes were just twigs with frayed ends. In some areas of the Middle East and Africa, similar tools are still used today – they're called miswaks and are made from twigs from the arak tree (also known as the toothbrush tree). The tip of the stick is soaked in hot water and then chewed so that the layers split and it forms something like a paintbrush. After brushing, the used part is cut off. The juices of the arak tree can help to fight bacteria, so the miswak acts as a toothbrush and toothpaste in one. In India, sticks from the neem tree, or Indian lilac, are sometimes used in a similar way.

The ancient Romans also used twigs. The Greeks apparently preferred to use cloth to clean their teeth. In Tudor England, Elizabeth I cleaned her teeth with handkerchiefs – quite elegant ones, as they were made of silk and trimmed with lace.

Ancient Egyptians used toothbrushes not unlike the ones we use today. The people of China likewise came up with the same solution. While their oldest tools probably looked more like paintbrushes, they also invented a toothbrush with bristles on one side, like a modern brush. They may have started using these tools way back in the 8th century CE, though some historians think they are more likely to date from the 15th century. In Europe, these tools were first used in France in the 16th century. At the end of the 18th century, William Addis opened the first toothbrush factory in east London. Apparently, the idea came to him when he was in prison, where he was serving time for starting a riot.

Mouthwash was also invented a long time ago. The ancient Greeks used extracts of camphor, cardamom and herbs or white wine with aniseed, dill and myrrh.

The Romans used to rinse their teeth with vinegar, and some historians think they may have even used pee as mouthwash.

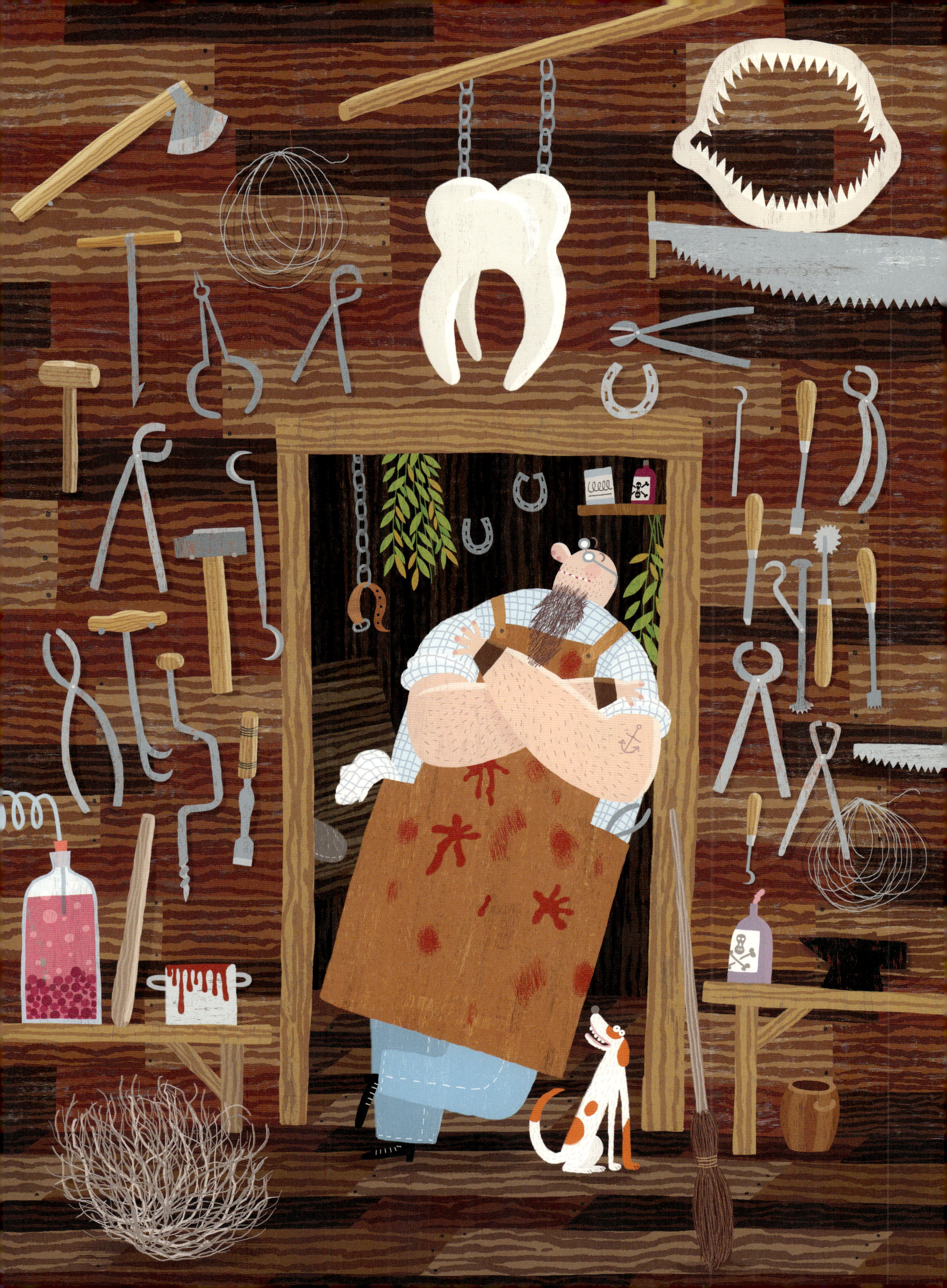

They definitely used urine as a bleach for fabrics, so they may well have believed that it would make their teeth whiter too. Much later, in the early 18th century, Pierre Fauchard, who is known as the father of French dentistry, really did recommend using pee as a mouthwash.

Over the centuries, various powders have been used instead of toothpaste. Delicate mixtures of this kind were used in ancient

Egypt. The ancient Romans were a little bit rougher when it came to cleaning their teeth – they made their tooth-cleaning powder from donkey bones, deer antlers, shells or chalk. Unluckily for them, this scratched and damaged their tooth enamel quite badly.

Toothpaste as we now know it was invented relatively recently. In 1850, an American dentist named Washington Sheffield added glycerol to a tooth-cleaning powder. At first, he sold the paste in jars but it quickly dried out when stored that way. The breakthrough came in 1892, when his son suggested using the kind of metal tubes that French artists used for their paint. The tube of toothpaste was born!

For a long time, many people believed that tooth decay was caused by bugs living inside the teeth. It was also blamed on demons – that's why the ancient Babylonians treated toothache with prayer and amulets. The people of ancient India, however, had quite modern tools for treating and removing teeth and tartar. These included bow-drills with hard stone tips that could be used to remove the rotten part of a tooth but leave the rest intact.

Dentistry was also relatively advanced in ancient Rome. The scholar Aulus Cornelius Celsus (1st century BCE) correctly thought that getting bits of food stuck between your teeth could cause *caries dentium* (dental cavities), and recommended daily tooth-brushing. His writings also include records of dental complaints and detailed instructions on how to pull a tooth out. What's more, he was probably the first person to ever fit a filling – he made it out of lead and lint cotton fibres.

Since the dawn of history, people have used to medicines to prevent pain. Celsus, who understood that toothache can be one of the most agonizing things, made a mixture from beavers' glands, mandrake, cinnamon and opium. In ancient Rome, Pliny the Elder recommended a mix of mice, rat, rabbit and wolf brains as a way to reduce swelling.

In later times, the Polish astronomer Nicolaus Copernicus (15th–16th centuries) recommended treating toothache with a mixture of alcohol and honey, pepper, celery seeds, rose flowers, pomegranate, burned coral and sugar. In the 16th century, the doctor and botanist Simon of Łowicz wrote: 'To treat a case of infested teeth,

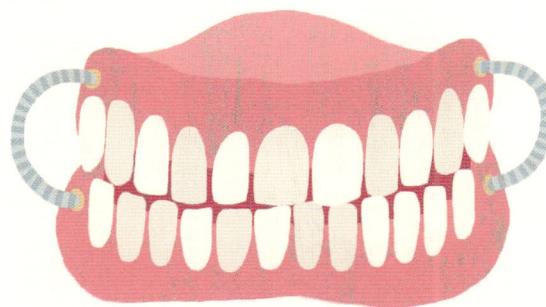

take some hemp seed, cook it in a new pot until it peels, then add nine hot stones. Lean over the steam and the bugs will fall out, naturally.'

Sometimes, however, nothing could be done and a tooth had to be pulled out. In the Middle Ages, this was mostly done by barber-surgeons and blacksmiths. The main job of a barber-surgeon was to cut hair and beards, but since they always had sharp tools, they often also let blood, which was once a common medical practice (see p. 83), and carried out minor surgical procedures. Many of them had little or no understanding of medicine, and some were just frauds who did their patients more harm than good.

Over the next few hundred years, not much progress was made in the art of pulling teeth. Louis XIV of France (17th century; see p. 79), often called on the services of a tooth-puller – by the age of forty, he was almost completely toothless. On one occasion, a barber-surgeon pulled out a tooth so hard that he damaged the king's jaw. As a result, Louis was left with a hole in his palate (the roof of his mouth). This meant that when he drank, wine poured out of his nose.

False teeth existed in ancient Rome – usually they were made of bone, hardwood or ivory. Later on, false teeth became more gruesome. The court dentist to Louis XV of Fance (18th century) would fill his patients' gaps with teeth from dead animals – or dead people! Sometimes, teeth were acquired from grave robbers. At the start of the 19th century, suppliers promised that they only sold teeth from Waterloo, the site of Napoleon's final battle. These teeth were extremely popular, because the dead soldiers were young and had healthy teeth. Porcelain false teeth were not invented until the 19th century.

However, if someone couldn't be bothered with all the rinsing and brushing, the barber-surgeons and dead men's teeth, they could always choose to hide their face behind a fan.

Wipe right

Toilet paper is a relatively recent invention. For centuries, people would use whatever they had to hand: grass, leaves, seaweed, moss, hay, wood shavings, wool, rags, sand, shells, stones, or snow. In America, they'd reach for corn husks (with the corn cob removed), and in the ruins of one ancient Egyptian town, archaeologists discovered a papyrus containing a commentary on Homer's poem *The Iliad*, stained with unmistakeable dirty marks!

The ancient Greeks wiped themselves using smooth stones or broken pieces of clay dishes. 'Three stones are enough,' they used to say – which meant more or less the same thing as 'You shouldn't use an entire roll in one go.' Apparently, it was quite popular to carve the names of your enemies into these pieces of pottery.

In the public toilets of ancient Rome (see p 110), a tool known as a *xylospongium* was used for wiping. This was a sponge on a long stick, dipped in vinegar or brine. Not a bad idea, perhaps, except that the sponge was probably reused and shared! The Roman toilet sponge plays an important role in a tragic tale, recorded in a letter by the writer Seneca: one German gladiator, who didn't want to die in the arena during a fight against wild animals, killed himself by shoving one of these sticks down his throat.

In China, for a long time, people would wipe themselves using a rag wrapped around a wooden or bamboo stick. This kind of tool has been discovered in a Chinese military camp from over two thousand years ago. We also know that similar sticks were used in ancient Japan.

In medieval Europe, people would apparently joke: 'What's the cleanest leaf in the forest? Holly – because nobody dares to wipe their bum on it!' Apart from leaves, moss, hay, straw and pieces of hide or fabric were popular choices. The rich would use soft wool, while the richest people would have special towels and handkerchiefs – as did the British and French royal families of the 15th, 16th and 17th centuries (see p. 118). The 18th-century French queen Marie Antoinette had a whole collection of lace hankies to do the job.

In a story by the French Renaissance writer François Rabelais, a giant called Gargantua describes wiping himself with various items of clothing (usually not his own). He also tries wiping himself with a cat (which scratches him terribly), a bedsheet, a blanket, curtains, a rug, a tablecloth, a pillow, a slipper, a basket (an awful idea), a chicken and a scarecrow, but he thought the best 'wipe-breech' was a live goose. Of course, we can't take the giant's list entirely seriously, but in the past, a bit of inventiveness really did go a long way.

Like ordinary paper, toilet paper was invented in China. Chinese people were probably using it by the 2nd century CE. Pieces of hemp paper, too rough to write on, were found in the tomb of one emperor from that period. In China, people also used normal paper for wiping. A Chinese scholar in the 6th century enjoyed the fact that he

had plenty of unwanted paper scraps for this purpose, but noted that he wouldn't dare use any paper with the words or names of wise men on it. Three hundred years later, an Arab traveller was surprised by the fact that after doing their business, Chinese people didn't wash but wiped themselves with paper. By the 15th century, toilet paper was quite common in China.

In Europe, normal paper was available by the 13th century, but it took a long time for people to start using it for wiping their bottoms. When Gargantua lists the various items he used as a wipe-breech, he says paper is no good because it doesn't clean his 'foul tail' properly.

The situation only changed in the 18th century, when newspapers and books became easily accessible. An 18th-century English earl wrote to his son that one of his friends tore out a few pages from a book by the Roman poet Horace every day, read them in the loo, then used them to wipe himself and 'sent them as a sacrifice to Cloacina', the Roman goddess of sewers (see p. 41). The earl advised his son to do the same – books read in this way were easier to remember, he claimed.

Telephone directories and magazines met a similar fate. In the United States, a handbook for farmers was particularly popular – it even had a hole in the corner so it could be hung on a hook in the bathroom. In the late 19th century, the department store Sears' catalogue, which also came with a punched hole in the corner, was often used in the same way. When the company began printing their catalogue on glossy paper in the early 20th century, they were flooded with complaints.

Modern-style toilet paper first appeared in 1857 – it took the form of large sheets sold in boxes, which the inventor

boasted were clean and protected against disease. Toilet roll was patented in the late 19th century, but at first its quality was rather poor. Even fifty years later, one American manufacturer was advertising its product as 'splinter-free', so presumably some brands must have been a bit rough!

Toilet paper is an everyday object but it can trigger strong feelings. What if it ran out, for instance? This prospect must have seriously horrified hundreds of people at the start of the COVID-19 pandemic – do you remember? When the countries of Eastern Europe were under Communist rule, toilet paper did occasionally run out. So when shops had some in stock, huge queues formed outside and people bought extra supplies.

But there are places around the world where toilet paper is almost never used. In Islamic countries, almost everyone washes themselves after going to the toilet, as well as or instead of wiping. Bathrooms there often have squat toilets – a ceramic or steel bowl in the floor, with a hole that you stand or squat over. Instead of a toilet roll holder, there's a shower attachment.

Many Japanese people also prefer washing to wiping, and they've invented some amazing technology to do it. It's called a washlet – a cross between a toilet and a bidet – and it washes your bum when you're finished. You can adjust the direction of the spray, temperature and pressure of the water using buttons on a special panel. There's also a hot-air dryer to dry you off.

No pain, no gain

The word 'spa' comes from the Belgian town of Spa, which has been a famous health resort since the 16th century. But the idea of water as a source of healing is even older. Hydrotherapy – the idea of using water and bathing to treat diseases – was popular back in ancient Greece and Rome.

This ancient art was revived in 17th-century Europe. Bathing places with mineral springs – like Bath in England, Vichy in France and Baden in Switzerland – were transformed from holiday spots into health centres (see p. 56). Wealthy people, aristocrats and the royals of Europe soon descended on them. People may not have washed to keep clean back then (see p. 87), but they did if they were told it was good for their health.

Today, we think of spas as places to relax and have fun, but in the 17th century, a visit to a spa was seen as an ordeal. Stays would last several weeks and take place under strict medical supervision. Patients had to wake up early in the morning and drink hot mineral water, which usually tastes disgusting. They also had to walk around to work up a sweat, and were often given a special diet. But the most important part of

the day was experiencing the baths, showers and water jets. One French aristocrat complained about the latter in particular. In a letter to her daughter, she described it as torture – it was embarrassing to strip naked, and uncomfortable to have hot water blasted at your body. 'But that's what it's all about,' she added. 'You have to suffer.'

In Britain in the late 17th and early 18th centuries, doctors began to promote the benefits of taking a cold bath, especially in the sea. They thought it was stimulating for the body and mind and would help people live longer. It was also used to treat illnesses, even serious ones like tuberculosis, paralysis, leprosy or blindness. In the mid-18th century, a centre was established in Brighton where patients could take a dip,

drink seawater and have seaweed massages. Soon this kind of therapy became popular across the whole country and later spread to France and beyond.

Sea baths were taken every day, though they didn't involve swimming (that was still quite a rare ability in those days). Instead, they involved soaking yourself in the water for around fifteen minutes. The colder the water, the better, so patients mostly went for treatments in autumn and winter. Young men went into the sea by themselves, while women and the elderly used bathing carriages – these were small wooden huts on four wheels, which were pulled into the water by horses. The patient would get changed inside (or undress, because at first people bathed in the nude), and then

opened the door and went down the steps into the water. Sometimes an attendant would even throw the patient into the waves or push their head under the water!

A 19th-century Austrian man named Vincenz Priessnitz is considered the founder of modern hydrotherapy. When he broke his ribs in an accident, he treated himself using only bandages soaked in cold water – at least, that's what he claimed. Doctors called him a fraud, but plenty of sick people believed him. In 1826, Vincenz opened a health resort and fifteen years later, he had hundreds of patients and was earning a fortune. The theory was simple – illnesses leave the body through the skin, so it must be thoroughly cleaned in order to open pores and boost circulation. For minor ailments, water was poured over the sick part of the body. When a patient's entire body was affected, they were wrapped in wet sheets for several hours.

Although this kind of therapy may seem a little strange to us now, health spas did do a lot to make the idea of bathing more popular with the public.

Squeaky clean

Attitudes towards water weren't the only thing that shifted in the late 18th century (see p. 148). Fashions also began to change – clothes became lighter, simpler and more revealing. Queen Marie Antoinette of France swapped her lavish gowns and tall powdered wigs (see p. 88) for plainer muslin dresses and straw hats. In a portrait from the 1780s, her hair is loose and lightly powdered and her make-up looks natural. Now that there was more of the body on show, people began paying more attention to hygiene.

Napoleon and his wife Josephine (18th–19th centuries) couldn't imagine a day without a long, hot bath. All their palaces had large bathrooms, sumptuously furnished, with luxurious tubs and bidets. During the emperor's morning wash, an aide would read him messages and newspapers. If he was dealing with a difficult political situation, his baths became longer and longer – the record was six hours. Napoleon was also famous for looking after his teeth; he brushed them regularly, used a boxwood

toothpick and had a whole set of tools for removing tartar.

One of the first and most famous European neat-freaks was George 'Beau' Brummell, born in London in 1778. He came from a middle-class family but believed he could turn himself into an aristocrat. In order to do this, he focused on practising good manners and elegance – and it worked! He became a member of high society and completely transformed ideas about men's fashion. It was thanks to him that the concept of style became associated with restraint and tidiness.

He didn't approve of gaudy colours, wigs, ribbons, lace or shoes with big buckles. 'If people notice you in the street,' he said, 'it means you're badly dressed.' Compared to the other fashionable men of his day, who usually wore very fancy outfits, he would dress very simply: a starched white shirt, an expertly-cut morning coat and trousers made from the best materials, with a white cravat and only a signet ring, pocket watch and cufflinks as accessories.

But above all, Brummell was always clean, shaved and perfumed. He spent a few hours every morning washing in warm water and scrubbing his whole body with a pig's-hair brush. Even when he was in prison, where he ended up because of his debts, he washed carefully every day and was always well groomed when he walked around the prison yard.

The 19th-century writer Charles Dickens was also a stickler for cleanliness. He was particularly fond of cold showers. His friends worried that this might be bad for his health, but he claimed that this kind of washing was very good for him – it toughened him up, reduced tiredness and helped his body recover. His house in London had a very modern bathroom with a tub and a shower. Once, when on holiday in the Isle of Wight, he even ordered a wooden cubicle to be built for him under a waterfall, so he could shower in it.

Clean inventions

In the centuries before homes had bathrooms with sinks and bathtubs or showers, people made do with a jug, a bowl and a washtub. Bathtubs were luxuries that very few could afford.

The world's oldest known bathtub is around 3,700 years old. It was discovered in a royal palace in Crete (see p. 115). The Polish king Władysław Jagiełło (14th–15th centuries) also had a tub – and not just any old tub, but one in the shape of a horse. Surprisingly, there were also bathtubs in Versailles (see p. 83). Louis XIV (17th century) had a luxurious bathroom built for himself, but instead of washing in it, he used it for meeting his lovers. Louis XV (18th century), however, used his bathtubs as intended – he would wash in one and rinse in the other.

However, Europe didn't yet have drains or sewers (see p. 99). Water had to be carried to the bathrooms and heated, and then taken away.

In the 19th century, a special service was invented for those who did not have servants but had a bit of money to spare. It was called *bain à domicile*, which means 'bath at home'. Clients were supplied with a tub, hot water, a dressing gown and towel, and then everything was removed once they were finished. Apparently, people would sometimes book a bath for somebody as

a joke, when they were in the middle of holding a party for instance, and the last thing they expected was a delivery team at their door with a portable bath.

Rich people weren't too fussed about installing bathrooms even when proper plumbing was available, because they could afford servants. In the late 19th century, some English castles still had water carriers, who spent their whole day wandering up and down staircases and corridors, topping up jugs and tubs in every bedroom.

By the late 19th century, everyone knew that staying clean was a way to stay healthy. Good hygiene became fashionable, and clever inventors tried to find new ideas for washing. One German designer came up with the *Wellenbadschaukel* – the cradle-bath. He advertised it as an alternative to a holiday at the seaside and as a way of cooling down on hot days. First you had to fill it with four buckets of water, then you got inside and rocked the bath gently backwards and forwards to make waves.

Another unusual invention was the steam box – a wooden cabinet that you could sit inside, with your head poking out through a hole in the top. The steam box, as its name suggests, was used for steam baths. According to its makers, it could strengthen the immune system, burned fat and was good for the skin, and they recommended it to treat all sorts of aches and pains.

The shower became popular at about the same time. The earliest versions were called shower-baths. The water came from a tank or a closed system of pipes – it was pumped up from the tub where the person was standing and sprayed out through a nozzle above their head. Inventors in the 19th century also tried to combine washing with exercise.

Frenchman Gaston Bozerian invented a shower-bath with a pump powered by foot pedals – it looked a bit like a modern-day cross-trainer at the gym. There was also a version powered by bike pedals. Later, somebody invented an unusual shower in the shape of a hoop worn around your neck, so you could shower while keeping your hair dry. By that time, it could be connected to a running water supply.

159

Barbarians from Europe

For many centuries, Europeans thought they were better than everyone else. But in fact, other cultures outranked them in many respects, including when it came to hygiene.

In the mid-20th century, the British writer Reginald Reynolds went to India and was asked what his religion taught about cleanliness. When he replied that it said practically nothing at all, the Indian people were astonished. Indeed, many religions give detailed advice about how to keep clean (see p. 59) but Christianity says very little.

In *The Arabian Nights*, an old Arab gardener says that Christians eat smelly food, drink a frothy yellow drink that smells of fermented urine (i.e. beer), and never wash.

(see p. 59)

At birth, revolting men in black robes pour water on their heads while making strange gestures, and that frees them from the need to wash for their entire lives.

Arabic authors from the time of the Crusades (see p. 43) called the Christian knights 'dirty pieces of rubbish' and 'human filth'. They wrote that the 'Franj' (the French) were full of courage, but had no other good points. They were dirty and behaved like wild animals. When the Arab ruler Saladin (12th century) conquered Jerusalem, he and his men personally scrubbed the Al-Aqsa mosque, which had been desecrated by the Crusaders. To do this, they used rose water specially brought from Damascus by Saladin's sister on the backs of camels.

The Europeans didn't make a very good impression in East Asia either. In the mid-16th century, when Portuguese sailors and traders reached Japan, they were called *nanbajin* – southern barbarians. Local writers recorded that they were impressed by the foreigners' knowledge, but noted with surprise that they were badly behaved, couldn't read and had no control over their emotions. But what they found most shocking was the European approach to hygiene. Many Japanese people washed at least once a day, kept their homes clean and frequently took steam baths. So they were horrified by the unshaven, smelly sailors in stained clothes who didn't know how to use chopsticks and preferred to eat with their filthy hands.

Hospital history

In modern hospitals and clinics, doctors and nurses always wear rubber gloves. Needles and syringes are only used once, and reusable equipment is always sterilized. But even in the early 19th century, this would never have crossed anyone's mind. Back then, not even surgeons washed their hands. At best, they'd wipe them on their aprons.

Hospitals at that time were overcrowded, stuffy and filthy. Nobody was surprised by lice or the stink of rotting wounds. The more sensitive doctors would cover their nose with a handkerchief. In these conditions, huge numbers of patients caught infections like gangrene or sepsis. These were fatal because antibiotics hadn't been discovered yet. Hospitals had a reputation as houses of death. As one British surgeon put it bluntly, you were more likely to survive on the battlefield.

This was all because people didn't know how illnesses spread. Some still believed they were caused by poisoned air (see p. 74). The first doctor to realize that hospital infections

were linked to poor hygiene was named Ignaz Semmelweis.

Semmelweis worked in a maternity hospital in Vienna, Austria. After giving birth, his patients often developed high temperatures and died. Semmelweis was deeply troubled by this, and spent a long time trying to work out why it happened. He had a brainwave in 1847, when a friend accidentally cut himself during a post-mortem, developed a fever and died. Ignaz realized that the medical students who came to the clinic for class had previously been practising in the morgue. The next day, he put up a notice on the door saying that every doctor and student had to wash their hands carefully in a bowl of chlorinated water before entering the hospital. His instinct was absolutely correct.

The death toll among his patients quickly fell to 1%.

Unfortunately, almost nobody paid attention to his findings. Ignaz tried very hard to get the message out – he published articles, wrote letters to medical authorities, and when that didn't help, he began kicking up a fuss and calling his opponents murderers – but none of it worked. Perhaps the doctors found it hard to accept that they were the ones infecting their patients with deadly diseases. One of the few people who did believe Semmelweis was so shocked that he took his own life.

In the 1860s, the British surgeon Joseph Lister started disinfecting wounds with phenol. He was also ignored at first, even though he saved many lives that way. The

situation did not change until a decade later, when the German doctor Robert Koch proved the existence of bacteria. But by then, Ignaz Semmelweis was dead. He had had a breakdown and ended up in a psychiatric hospital, where he was killed by an infection – exactly the thing he'd fought so hard against.

Florence Nightingale played an important role in improving hospital hygiene. As a girl, she decided to become a nurse. Her parents didn't approve, because back then it was a job often associated with drunkards and criminals. But Florence got her own way and began working in a London hospital in 1853. A year later, at the head of a 38-strong team of nurses, she went to care for wounded British soldiers in the Crimean War.

When she first arrived, the conditions in the field hospital were horrendous. It was stuffy and dirty and there were shortages of everything – bandages, medicines, even beds. Patients were often simply laid on the floor. Florence began by ordering the windows to be opened and buying three hundred brooms. Together with her team, she scrubbed everything clean. Next, she set up a laundry and kitchen, where they cooked healthy meals for the sick. The nurses kept everything clean, gave out medicines and changed bandages, but they also cared about their patients, reading to them and helping them to write letters to their families. At first, the doctors viewed Florence with mistrust, but the facts spoke for themselves. Thanks to the work of her nurses, the patient death rate dropped from 40% to 2%.

Washing without washing

There are plenty of people in the world who wash without soap. Others don't even use water. There are even some who don't really have to wash at all.

The Himba people live in northwest Namibia in southern Africa. Traditionally they are shepherds, breeding goats and cows. They live in small mud huts without electricity or running water, so they have to carry water to their villages in jugs. Water is so hard to find in the Namibian desert that

they use it only for drinking. That's why the Himba wash with sand and smoke. They place hot ashes, resins and herbs in a dish and then apply the smoke to themselves. They clean their clothes this way as well.

Himba women also spread *otjize*, a special cream of butter, plant oils, ash and a type

of reddish clay called ochre, on their body and hair. They do this for beauty purposes – it's a kind of make-up. But *otjize* also has other advantages – it tones and smooths the skin and protects it from bacteria, fungus, insects and the sun.

The Jain monks and nuns of India do not wash either, but for different reasons. Jains believe in reincarnation (being reborn in a new body after death) and that you can free yourself from the cycle of reincarnation by being a good person (see p. 64). One of the most important principles in Jainism is *ahinsa* – non-violence towards all living things. For this reason, Jains don't eat meat or use items made of bone or leather, and they often run shelters and hospitals for animals. Jain monks sweep the ground in front of them with special brushes so that they don't step on any tiny creatures as they walk. Some also cover their mouths with masks to avoid accidentally swallowing insects. Because of the Jains, there is also an official ban on eating and selling meat and eggs in Palitana, a city that contains hundreds of Jain temples.

As well as trying not to harm anyone or anything, Jain monks and nuns are also

ascetics (see p. 50) – this means that they give up all possessions and comforts. They don't use modern inventions, they walk barefoot (some don't even wear clothes), and they only eat what they receive from others. What's more, they don't wash or use soap – not in the sea, in lakes or rivers, or in the bath or shower. Instead, they just wipe their skin with a wet cloth.

There are also some people in the world who could easily choose to never wash, because they don't smell. They have a genetic mutation that means that their sweat doesn't contain the ingredients that bacteria feed on, and these chemicals are what make up the 'sweaty' smell we recognize– even though sweat itself basically smells of nothing at all.

What's the wax like in your ears? Is it sticky and damp, or is it crusty and dry? If it's the latter, you're a lucky carrier of this mutation. But if you come from Europe or Africa, the chances of having it are small – around 2%. It's much more common in northeast Asia, however. It's estimated that over 90% of people in countries from that region, including Korea and China, have odourless sweat and dry earwax.

A world of differences

'Health', 'purity', 'hygiene' – these all sound like good things, don't they? But these words can also have very sinister meanings.

Have you ever heard people say things like 'British people are so polite' or 'Men are bad at housework'? These are stereotypes – frequently shared, simplified opinions about certain groups of people. Stereotypes aren't based on observation or knowledge, just on repetition – and they're untrue, because in reality people are very different. You don't have to look hard to find someone who doesn't fit a stereotype!

If stereotypes are about positive characteristics, that's not a big problem. Unfortunately, they're often used to say negative things about groups of people,

such as claiming everyone from that group is stupid or lazy. And from there, it's a quick path to prejudice (unjustified dislike) and discrimination (unfair treatment).

This is a very serious problem. Millions of people across the whole world face discrimination. They have trouble finding good jobs, they're not respected or listened to, they're denied their basic rights, and they're made to suffer violence – and sometimes even imprisonment, torture and death.

People often repeat stereotypes without thinking, just because that's what they've always heard and they take these statements for granted. But stereotypes can also be spread, maintained and fuelled by people who benefit from them – because it helps them to boost their own status or to justify exploiting people they believe are 'inferior' to them.

One of the most common forms of prejudice is racism, the belief that some 'races' of humans are better than others. It began to spread around the world in the late 15th century, when Europeans set out to conquer other continents. In this way,

countries such as Spain and Portugal, and later Great Britain and France, became colonial empires. They used violence to invade lands overseas (which they called colonies), imposed their power on the local people and took their riches. To justify this, the colonizers said native people belonged to savage and inferior 'races', while they, the whites, were bringing them civilization.

One example of this kind of thinking was the poem 'The White Man's Burden'. It was written in 1899 by the British author Rudyard Kipling. The poem says that white people have an obligation to pass on their knowledge, teach morality and treat illnesses and famine in these countries – but they have to accept the fact that it'll be a thankless task. Poor them, eh?

Overwhelmed by his duty towards the rest of the world, a symbolic white man also appeared in a 19th-century poster advertising soap. Underneath a picture of a gentleman in a pale suit washing his hands, the slogan said: 'The first step towards lightening the white man's burden is through teaching the virtues of cleanliness. Pears'

Soap is a potent factor in brightening the dark corners of the earth.'

Between the 16th and 18th centuries, white people kidnapped millions of Africans and took them to America, which they had conquered, and forced them to work as slaves. Slaves were treated as if they were objects, not people. Slave owners could do anything they liked with them, even kill them – and they faced no punishment. Racist stereotypes meant that they believed they had every right to do this.

In 1865, slavery was abolished in the USA and white and Black people were officially declared equal – but prejudices remained. The recently freed African Americans were very poor and had no money for education. Without it, they couldn't get better jobs so they remained poor. Looking at them, white people thought their prejudiced opinions must be true – now that Black people were free, why had they still not become scientists, doctors or lawyers? If a Black person did manage to receive an education, the same white people, still driven by their prejudices, would refuse to give them a job. These racist ideas were so deeply rooted that in the late 19th and early 20th century, the principle of white and Black being 'separate but equal' was allowed by the American courts. This led to racial segregation in the southern states of the USA. White and Black children went to separate schools, and there were also separate hotels, restaurants, shops, and even park benches. This lasted until the 1960s. One famous figure in the fight against racial segregation was Rosa Parks. She was a Black woman who broke the racist rules in 1955 and refused to give a white person her seat on a bus when all the 'white' places were occupied.

Racial segregation also existed between the 1940s and the 1990s in the Republic of South Africa. There it was called *apartheid*, which means 'separateness' in the language of Afrikaans.

Negative stereotypes often include references to health and hygiene. Sometimes these are literal – for instance, people are said to be dirty, to live in filthy places and spread illnesses, or they're compared

to disease-spreading animals like rats, cockroaches, fleas or lice. Sometimes it's a symbolic idea – like when people talk about the cleanliness or purity of a 'nation', 'blood' or 'race'.

In Europe in the 1920s and 1930s, an idea called eugenics became popular – this was the so-called 'science' of breeding humans to make them 'better'. It was invented by a British man named Francis Galton, who believed that all physical and mental features were inherited. He thought that healthy and talented people should be encouraged to have lots of children for the good of society. At the same time, Galton believed that it should be made more difficult for sick and immoral people to have babies. In many European countries, organizations were set up to promote these views.

Adolf Hitler was one of the people who believed some 'races' were better than others. He thought the superior 'race' was the 'Aryan' one, which included most Germans. He also believed that when people of different 'races' had children together, it made the 'superior' ones less pure. His plan was to let Aryans have lots of children, while at the same time, sterilizing and killing people with diseases and disabilities. He also wanted the Aryans to conquer and kill people he thought were 'inferior', such as Jews, Romani and Slavs. You probably know what happened next from history class.

Racists often tried to use science to explain their prejudices. However, it was the science of genetics that showed that the very idea of 'race' is nonsense. But although we know this now, and although the old colonial empires have disappeared and slavery and segregation have been abolished, prejudice and discrimination have not. To make things worse, white people are often completely unaware of this or simply refuse to understand it.

No matter what colour your skin is, remember that the fight against racism is also yours. Don't think in shortcuts. Don't believe stereotypes, don't repeat them, and remember to speak out if somebody else does. Every person is different – and everyone is equal.

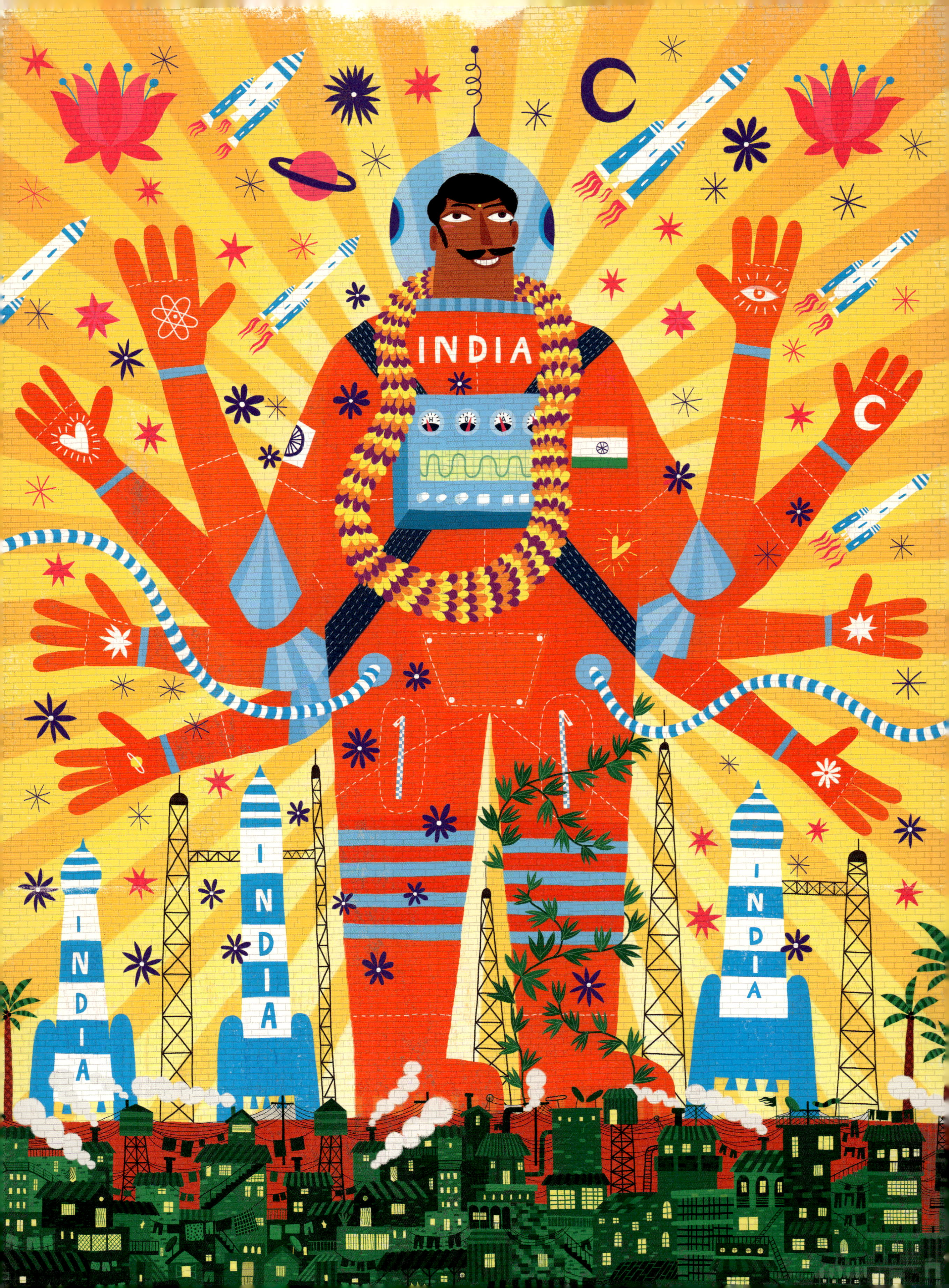
INDIA
INDIA
INDIA
INDIA

Rockets and toilets

Can you imagine a life without toilets? For some people, it's an everyday reality. According to the World Health Organization, nearly 700 million people still have to relieve themselves in the open air.

Most of them live in poorer countries in southern Africa and Asia that were once ruled by colonial empires (see p. 176). With no toilets, people have to do their business in bushes, rivers, by roadsides and train tracks or in fields. Where toilets and sewers do exist, there is often no proper treatment of sewage. Waste flows straight into lakes, rivers and seas, gutters and streets, and it poisons the soil and water.

India is one country that faces problems like these. It is an amazing country. More than 1.3 billion people live there – almost as many as in China, the most populous country in the world, which is three times bigger in size. The Indian economy is growing at a huge speed – it may soon be the third largest on the planet, after the USA and China. India is also home to cutting-edge technology – it even has its own space programme,

and the research that it carries out is vital in a country that's reliant on monsoons and has a huge farming population. In 2008, they sent a probe into orbit around the moon that confirmed the presence of water there, and in 2014, an Indian probe went into orbit around Mars. What's more, the Indian space telescope Astrosat has been circling the Earth since 2015.

India can also boast about another huge success on a less cosmic scale. In 2014, over half a billion Indian people did not have access to a toilet – that's almost half the population. Today, that number is only around 50 million – a massive improvement.

For years, India struggled with poor sanitation and the diseases it causes. The main problem was a lack of toilets. When people relieve themselves in the open air, flies rapidly spread the bacteria, viruses and parasites contained in their poo. Every year, tens of thousands of Indian children died from diarrhoea, and many more suffered from diseases.

The second problem was polluted water. The Ganges, the main source of water for

half of all Indian people, is one of the dirtiest rivers in the world. It's filled not only with polluted sewage from cities and factories, but also dead bodies (see p. 64). It's estimated that the river contains around 200 tonnes of decomposing remains.

The famous Indian politician and thinker Mahatma Gandhi understood the seriousness of the situation. In the 1920s, he used to say that sanitation was more important than independence. One of the first people who took his words to heart was the sociologist Bindeshwar Pathak. In 1970, he set up the charity Sulabh International, which works to promote human rights and build cheap toilets. Today it boasts 50,000 volunteers, making it the largest non-profit organization in India.

Indian society is traditionally divided into groups called castes. At the bottom of the list of castes are the Dalits. They are considered 'unclean', so often face discrimination (see p. 176) and are forced to do 'dirty' jobs such as rubbish collection, butchery or cleaning sewers. Pathak is a Brahmin – a member of a social class that does more intellectual work

– but he has fought for years to improve the lives of the Dalits. His foundation, Sulabh International, helps them find better jobs and works to ensure that cleaning sewers by hand is not necessary. To do this, it has invented a simple, cheap and eco-friendly flushing toilet that doesn't have to be emptied. Sulabh International has now built over 1.5 million toilets. Some of these toilet buildings include bathrooms and equipment that can generate electricity from biogas. The public toilets that the charity has built in densely populated areas of Indian cities are used by ten million people every day.

Politicians are also working to solve the toilet problem. During his election campaign, the current Prime Minister of India, Narendra Modi, adopted the slogan: 'Toilets first, temples later!' The first phase of his 'Clean India' mission began in 2014 and ended in October 2019, on the 150th anniversary of Gandhi's birth. In five years, Modi's government paid for the building of over 100 million toilets. UNICEF, which is a partner of the programme, says that by early 2020, over 600,000 Indian villages were 'open defecation free' – this means that nobody had to do their business in the open air any more.

And that's not all. In 2021, India wants to send another probe to the moon and is planning its first manned space mission, in which three Indian astronauts will spend around a week orbiting the Earth. If they manage it, India will become the fourth country – after the USA, China and Russia – to achieve this on their own. Preparations for this new mission are taking place at the same time as the second phase of the sanitation programme, which will end in 2025.

In orbit

Around 400 kilometres above our heads, the International Space Station has been orbiting the Earth since 1998. The station has had astronauts living in it since the start of the 21st century. Usually, teams of six people live there for six months at a time. So far, more than two hundred astronauts from around twenty countries have spent time there.

The station travels at a speed of 7.7 kilometres per second – it takes an hour and a half to orbit the Earth. This means that the astronauts inside can see sixteen sunsets every day.

There's no gravity inside the station – people and objects float around, as if they were swimming in the air. In a place like this, doing even the most ordinary activities is very different. Instead of walking, the astronauts move around by pushing themselves off walls. When they sleep, they float inside sleeping bags tied to the wall. If they want to run on a treadmill, they have to attach themselves to it using a special harness. In these conditions, you can't have a bath

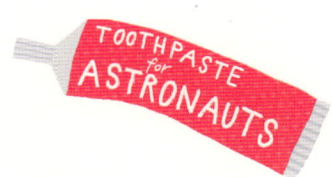

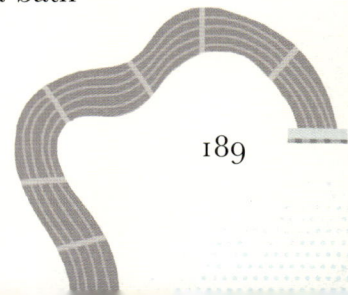

TOOTHPASTE for ASTRONAUTS

or take a shower in the usual way. Firstly, there's not much water on the International Space Station because it's very expensive to transport it up there. Instead, astronauts must save it and recycle it. Every drop of water – including sweat, wet towels and even the astronauts' breath – is sucked in by the ventilation system, cleaned and used again. Secondly, in a weightless environment, water from a tap or shower would form lots of floating blobs. That's why there aren't any showers or taps in the station. Instead, there are special bags or sachets

with a tube and valve that can be filled with water from dispensers.

Astronauts wash by wiping themselves with a small towel moistened with water and liquid soap. They can also squeeze water and soap from a sachet straight onto their skin and rub it in, but they must be careful not to splash the water around. Space soap doesn't create much foam so it doesn't need to be rinsed off – just dried with a towel.

Space shampoo doesn't need rinsing either. To wash their hair, astronauts wet it with water from a sachet, rub in the shampoo and then dry it with a towel. But brushing your teeth is almost exactly the same as on Earth – with only one difference. There are no sinks for spitting out the toothpaste. Some astronauts spit their toothpaste into a towel, others prefer to swallow it.

In a place where everything floats in the air, how do you go to the toilet? Well, a space toilet is basically a kind of vacuum cleaner. There's a special suction tube with a funnel for peeing, and a toilet that's quite similar to an Earth one, except that it also sucks the poo away. Before you do your business, you have to put a special plastic bag inside the toilet, to collect the poo. Afterwards, the bag goes into a container underneath the toilet. When the container is full, it's put in a special bin that's sent back towards Earth and burns up as it enters the atmosphere. Urine, however, is filtered and purified by a machine that recovers the water from it. That's why astronauts joke that today's coffee will be tomorrow's coffee too!

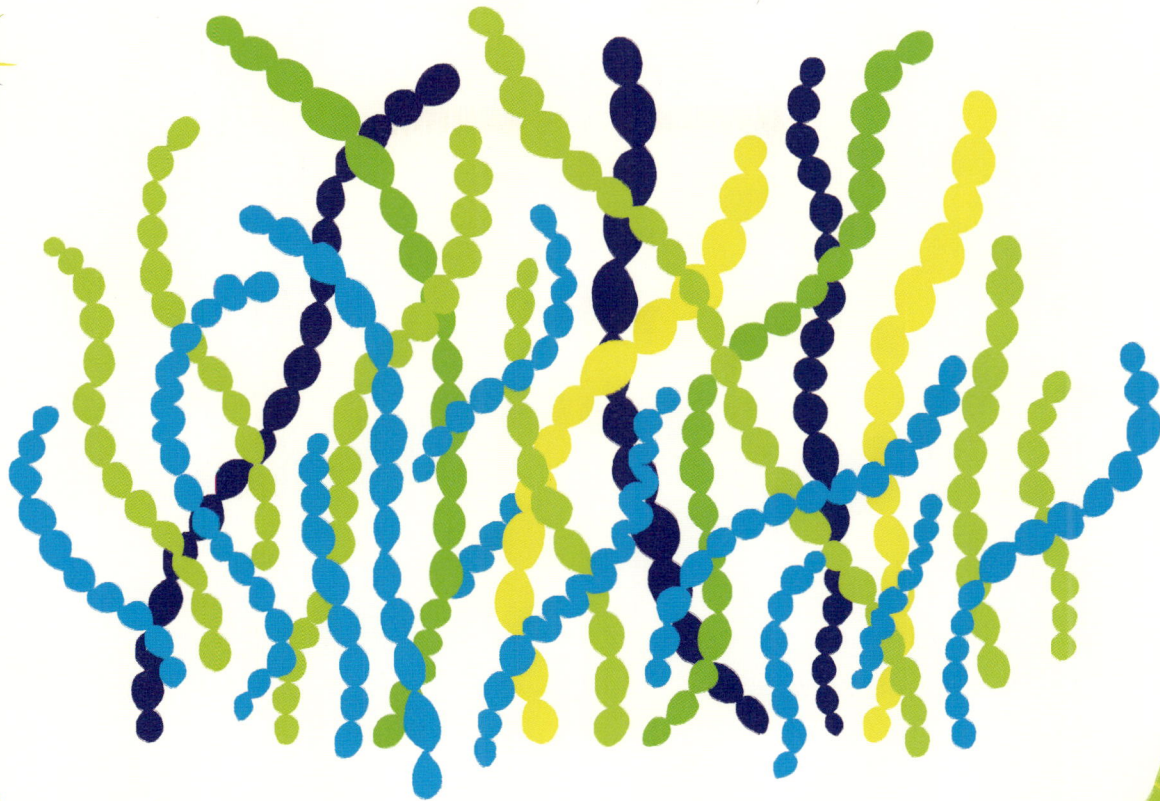

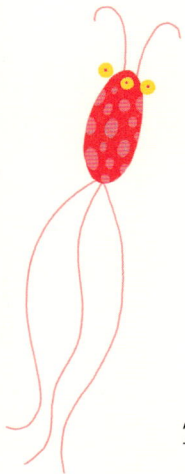

Bacteria can save the world!

The War of the Worlds by H.G. Wells is one of the best-known science-fiction novels ever. It was published in the late 19th century and has been adapted many times. In 1938, the actor Orson Welles made a famous radio version of the story. American newspapers claimed it was so realistic that some people thought aliens really were invading the planet and started to panic – but sadly that tale isn't true.

In *The War of the Worlds*, Wells describes how aliens from Mars arrive to invade the Earth (spoiler alert!).

Picture the scene. It's the early 20th century and mysterious capsules start falling out of the sky and landing in a quiet English town. The capsules contain aliens – huge grey creatures, a bit like octopuses – and unfortunately, they haven't come to make friends. They build massive war machines that look like three-legged spiders and create death and destruction using poisonous gases and a kind of laser. Humans don't stand a chance against them. In no

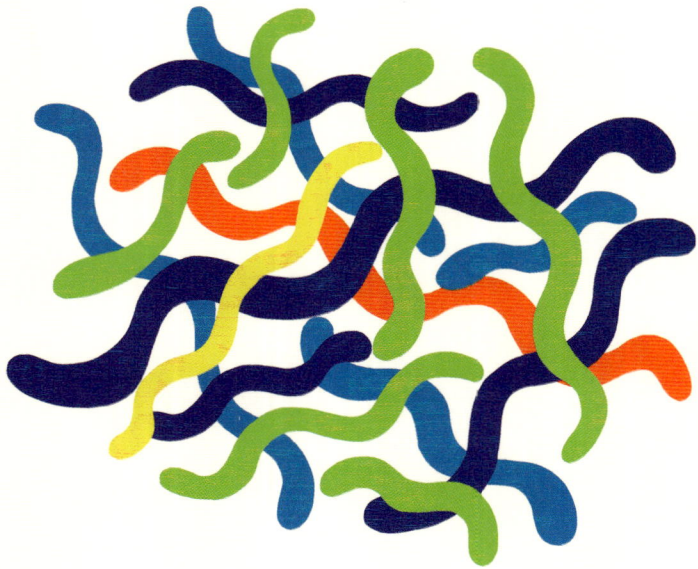

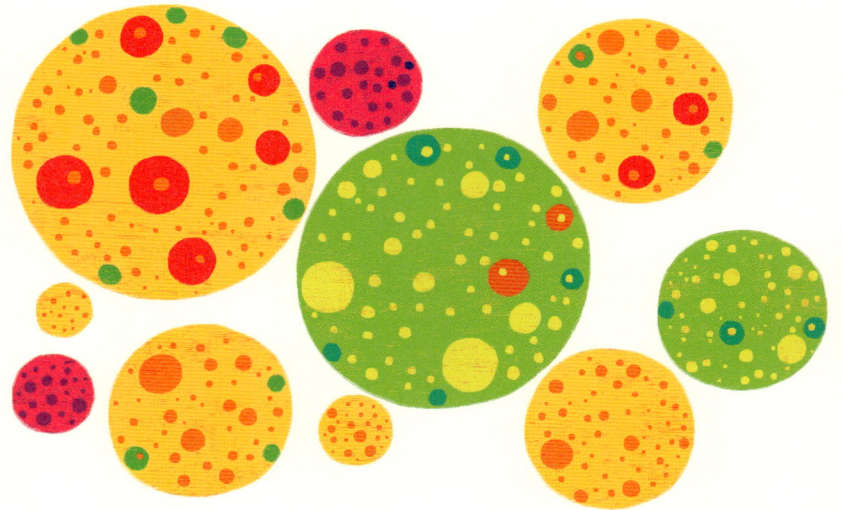

time at all, the Martians take control of London and the surrounding area. But then, after barely two weeks on our planet, they all suddenly die. Why? Well, they may have been ultra-intelligent with much better technology than the human race, but they weren't immune to our diseases. They were killed by Earth's bacteria. The Martians' weakness was because their own planet was sterile. They'd never come into contact with bacteria before, which is vital for building up immunity. The body has to encounter the enemy in order to learn how to fight against it.

Hygiene is hugely important for our health, but too much of it can be harmful. That's why some doctors say that young children shouldn't have a bath every day.

Around 2,000 different types of microorganisms, known as microbes, live in the human body and on the skin. The average young adult has about 39 trillion bacteria inside them – around 9 trillion more than there are cells in the body. If it were possible to take them out, they would weigh a total of 2 kilograms.

Bacteria can be found in our guts, in our noses and mouths, on our skin – all over us, in fact. Over one hundred microorganisms live on one square centimetre of our skin. One millilitre of saliva (spit) contains 10 billion of them. Our teeth are covered in a layer of bacteria, several hundred cells thick – the more sugar we eat, the thicker it gets. One gram of poo contains over a thousand microorganisms. The collection

of microorganisms living on one body is called a microbiome.

This might be a scary thought, but most of these tiny organisms are harmless, and some are even our friends. In fact, without many of them, our bodies would not work properly. Our microbiome protects our body from bacteria and fungi that can cause diseases. It also helps us to digest our food and even makes certain vitamins.

This may result in a problem if we take too many antibiotic drugs. These are designed to kill harmful bacteria but can also destroy the useful ones if taken in very large quantities. If we forget to support the 'good' microorganisms by eating pro-biotics (they are often added to yoghurt), it can help the harmful kind, and we might suffer stomach upsets or other illnesses as a consequence.

Does your skin sometimes feel itchy after taking a bath? It might be because you're washing too much. Our skin is covered in a layer of dead cells and living bacteria called sebum. Sebum acts as a protective shield. If we scrub our skin too hard, the layer of sebum can't rebuild itself and so the skin becomes dry, itchy and cracked. This makes it easier for bad bacteria to attack. Washing our hair too often can have a similar effect.

As with many other things in life, the best solution is to find a middle way – a happy medium. Of course. it's important to care about hygiene (especially washing our hands), but there's no need to go too far!

Principal sources

Alberto Angela, *A Day in the Life of Ancient Rome*, translated by Gregory Conti, 2009

Katherine Ashenburg, *The Dirt on Clean: An Unsanitized History*, 2007

Mary Beard, *Pompeii: The Life of a Roman Town*, 2008

Lindsey Fitzharris, *The Butchering Art: Joseph Lister's Quest to Transform the Grisly World of Victorian Medicine*, 2017

Sextus Julius Frontinus, *Aqueducts of Rome*, translated by C.E. Bennett, 1925

Yuval Noah Harari, *Sapiens: A Brief History of Humankind*, 2014

Robert Hughes, *Rome: A Cultural, Visual and Personal History*, 2011

Mieczysław Jesionowski, *The History of Polish Dentistry* (in Polish), 1963

Arnold van de Laar, *Under the Knife: A History of Surgery in 28 Remarkable Operations*, 2018

Anthony Levi, *Louis XIV*, 2004

Victoria Sherrow, *Encyclopedia of Hair: A Cultural History*, 2006

Wojciech Ślusarczyk (ed.), *The History of Hygiene Written in Water* (in Polish), 2017

Jürgen Thorwald, *The Century of the Surgeon*, translated by Richard and Clara Winston, 1957

Georges Vigarello, *Concepts of Cleanliness: Changing Attitudes in France since the Middle Ages*, translated by Jean Birrell, 1988

Marcin Winkowski, *When Poles Wore Dreadlocks: A True Story* (in Polish), 2019

James Wynbrandt, *The Excruciating History of Dentistry: Toothsome Tales & Oral Oddities from Babylon to Braces*, 1998

Quotation sources

Quotes on pages 8–11: Katherine Ashenburg, *The Dirt on Clean: An Unsanitized History*; Eleanor Herman, *The Royal Art of Poison: Fatal Cosmetics, Deadly Medicines and Murder Most Foul*; Aldous Huxley, *Brave New World*; Mieczysław Jesionowski, *A History of Polish Dentistry*; Ovid *The Art of Love*, translated by A.S. Kline; Georges Vigarello, *Concepts of Cleanliness: Changing Attitudes in France since the Middle Ages*, translated by Jean Birrell.

Quote from the Gospel according to St Matthew on p. 14 is from the New King James Version.

Quote from *On Good Manners for Boys* by Erasmus of Rotterdam on pp. 133–134 is from Katherine Ashenburg, *The Dirt on Clean: An Unsanitized History*.

Originally published in 2021 under the title *Brud. Cuchnąca historia higieny*
by Wydawnictwo Dwie Siostry, Warsaw.

Translated from the Polish by Zosia Krasodomska-Jones

First published in the United Kingdom in 2022 by
Thames & Hudson Ltd, 181A High Holborn, London WC1V 7QX

British Library Cataloguing-in-Publication Data
A catalogue record for this book is available from the British Library

ISBN 978-0-500-65266-4

Printed in Poland